THE
COMPLETE POEMS
AND SELECTED LETTERS
AND PROSE OF
HART CRANE

THE

COMPLETE POEMS

AND SELECTED LETTERS

AND PROSE OF

HART CRANE

EDITED WITH AN

INTRODUCTION AND NOTES BY

BROM WEBER

ANCHOR PRESS
Doubleday

NEW YORK   LONDON   TORONTO   SYDNEY   AUCKLAND

Some of the material collected in the present edition and used by permission of the Hart Crane Estate was first published in book form as follows:

Hart Crane: A Biographical and Critical Study, by Brom Weber, Bodley Press, New York, 1948. Copyright 1948 by Brom Weber.

Hart Crane: The Life of an American Poet, by Philip Horton, W. W. Norton & Company, Inc., New York, 1937. Copyright 1937 by W. W. Norton & Company, Inc.

Twice a Year: A Book of Literature, the Arts, and Civil Liberties, Volumes 13-14, Twice a Year Press, New York, 1945. Copyright 1945 by Dorothy S. Norman, *Twice a Year*.

The publishers wish to thank Samuel Loveman for his assistance and co-operation.

The Complete Poems and Selected Letters and Prose of Hart Crane was originally published in a hardbound edition by Liveright Publishing Corp. in 1966. The Anchor Books edition is published by arrangement with Liveright Publishing Corp.

To Waldo Frank
Constant Friend of Hart Crane

CONTENTS

TWO · THE BRIDGE

THREE · UNCOLLECTED POEMS

FOUR · SELECTED PROSE

INTRODUCTION

A new, revised edition of Hart Crane's distinguished poetry is necessary now. Both the *Collected Poems* (1933) and its 1958 reprinting (*Complete Poems*) are out of print. Since 1933, many new poems that did not appear in the first collected edition have been uncovered in manuscripts and periodicals. In addition, the texts appearing in *Collected Poems* and *Complete Poems* were not always correct.

Thirty-three years ago, when Crane's friend Waldo Frank undertook to assemble the first collection, it was equally essential to get such a volume into print, though for different reasons. An unwarranted shadow had been cast over Crane's artistry and achievement by the sensational circumstances of his death by drowning in April 1932, the grim belief shared by himself and others that he had lost his poetic powers, the less-than-enthusiastic reception accorded his last book (*The Bridge*, 1930), and his partial repudiation by those who had praised his earlier work in *White Buildings* (1926) and had been linked with him as members of a major school of modern American poets. Attention was diverted to Crane the man, a symbolic figure cited in diverse ways by those polemicizing about romanticism, capitalism, humanism, mysticism, optimism, and other cultural concerns of large character. Frank's timely edition decisively saved the poet from the fate of becoming merely a polemical resource and buttressed the continued life of his writings.

Of course, the brilliance of Crane's poetry ensured its ultimate survival even had it been concealed in scarce out-of-print volumes and not generously exposed so soon. In addition, the poetry's temper and rhetoric proved irresistibly appealing to some of the most significant poets of the post-1920s, men of Crane's generation such as Horace Gregory and younger men such as Robert Lowell, Dylan Thomas, Karl Shapiro, and John Berryman.

Meanwhile, too, even during its heyday the authority of critics oriented in the "traditional modernism" expounded by Cleanth Brooks in *Modern Poetry and the Tradition* (1939) had begun to wane. Such critics had tended generally to acknowledge Crane's powers, but to conclude that he had used them unwisely in *The Bridge* and thus essentially had failed.

Brooks's procedure in dealing with Crane is symptomatic. In one chapter, Brooks provided a "scaffolding" for T. S. Eliot's rehabilitation of a dormant myth in *The Waste Land;* in another chapter Brooks discussed W. B. Yeats's creation of a new myth. Nevertheless, though Brooks granted that Crane "possessed one of the most brilliant talents of his generation, and some of his poems are surely among the most brilliant of our time," and though Crane had undertaken in *The Bridge* the unique dual task of criticizing the myth of untraditional "modernism" and substituting for it a new myth of his own construction, *Modern Poetry and the Tradition* had no place for an extended criticism of Crane. As Brooks put it, Crane's "omission from this study is based on a general consideration of the clarity of the book as a whole—not certainly on his lack of importance as a poet." The impression conveyed was that the question of Crane had been settled earlier in the 1930s.

Ironically, younger critics imbued with the passion for concrete analysis encouraged by Brooks and his colleagues, increasingly grew discontented with definitive judgments disposing of Crane that were not strengthened by continued critical scrutiny. As early as 1937, Philip Horton's biography of Crane presented an essentially favorable portrait of a romantic poet. My own critical-biographical study of 1948 maintained an evaluative equilibrium between negative judgment of *The Bridge* as a long poem and high praise for the poet's lyrical genius and successes. In "Symbolism in *The Bridge*" (PMLA, March 1951), Stanley K. Coffman wrote the first of a number of articles by American critics which champion the unity, structure, and method of *The Bridge*.

The revisionist approach to Crane was accelerated by the publication of his letters in 1952, for these fascinating documents display an intelligence, knowledge, perspicuity, and range that even his closest intimates seem to have slighted or overlooked. Since 1952, books and monographs on Crane by Lawrence S. Dembo, Samuel Hazo, Vincent Quinn, and Monroe K. Spears, as well as sections of books by Robert J. Andreach, Glauco Cambon, James E. Miller, Karl Shapiro, and Bernice Slote, have firmly fixed the importance and high quality of Crane's poetry in the canon of American letters. It is pleasing to observe that the traditional destructive pattern of hasty neglect and overdue revival, which for long periods deprived American culture of Herman Melville, Emily Dickinson, and Henry James, has not been effective in Hart Crane's case.

Although Crane's reputation has continued to grow ever greater, it is still encumbered with hangovers of the ideological and literary conflicts of the twenties and thirties that momentarily obscured his poetic worth. Perhaps the most dire effect is the excessive emphasis placed upon *The Bridge* as the fulcrum upon which judgment of the poet must be based. The emphasis is historically understandable, for it was that poem which separated Crane from most of his friends and erstwhile critical supporters, dividing them into two camps: those—a majority—who favored *White Buildings* over *The Bridge,* and the small minority which reversed that order of partiality. Recently some critics have even come to believe that only a complete reversal of the formerly dominant negative attitude toward *The Bridge* will enable Crane's reputation to rest secure.

The Bridge may ultimately be regarded as Crane's supreme individual achievement. In the meantime, however, an unwarranted slighting of his other poems is occurring that may be hardening into an attitude perhaps as single-minded as the one which formerly dismissed *The Bridge* with mechanical regularity. Truly this is regrettable, for some of Crane's finest poems and lines thus tend to be ignored. Crane himself, as it happens, did not believe that his worth appeared only or primarily in *The Bridge.*

The occasion of a new edition of Crane's poetry, designed to replace the *Collected Poems* of 1933 and its 1958 reissue under the title of *Complete Poems,* provides an opportunity to set forth the body of work in a manner encouraging fresh consideration of all the poems, those preceding and following *The Bridge* as well as that poem itself. Because Waldo Frank strongly admired *The Bridge* and considered that *White Buildings* lacked a significant theme, he gave first place in *Collected Poems* to *The Bridge.* In the present edition the earlier *White Buildings* precedes *The Bridge.* Poems not included in either of those two volumes have been assembled here as Uncollected Poems. This section has been arranged in chronological order based on known or conjectured dates of composition; however, the order of poems in Crane's tentative table of contents for "Key West: An Island Sheaf," his projected third book, has been followed without concern for the resulting violation of chronological order. The dates of first appearance in print of the uncollected poems will be found at the bottom right of the poems.

This new edition adds seventeen poems not in *Collected Poems*. Most of the poems added were written before 1926 and published in magazines. "C 33," Crane's first known published poem, is part of that group. The rest of the added poems have been taken from authenticated manuscripts; among them is Crane's earliest known poem, "The Moth That God Made Blind," written in 1915.

The present collection has been planned as a "reader's edition," with a variorum edition projected for the future. Accordingly, several items that properly belong in a variorum edition have been excluded. They fall into several categories: early drafts of poems included in the present volume, fragmentary lines, poems of preponderantly unfinished character, and poems whose authorship by Crane is questionable. The pieces in *Collected Poems* excluded here are "The Tree: Great William" (early draft), "The Return" (fragment), "A Traveler Born" (unfinished poem), "Enrich My Resignation" (unfinished poem), and "The Circumstance" (unfinished poem). Poetry either collected elsewhere or still in manuscript likewise has not been included here if it belongs in the categories warranting exclusion.

Contrary to Waldo Frank's assertion in *Collected Poems* (p. [162]) that Crane "destroyed the manuscripts" of poems written before 1919 that he did not insert in *White Buildings*, a notebook in the Hart Crane Collection in Columbia University Libraries reveals that Crane preserved at least two such poems ("Postscript" and "Forgetfulness"). Furthermore, the notebook also contains final versions of many poems composed between 1919 and 1926 which were not included in *White Buildings*. This suggests that Crane believed much of his early poetry worthy of preservation, if not of inclusion in his first book, and has led to its appearance in the pages which follow.

Probably the most important feature differentiating the present edition from *Collected Poems* consists of the re-edited texts of poetry and prose appearing in the 1933 book. For example, errors in punctuation, language, stanza spacing, and the like which violated the poet's last authoritative text or impaired his meaning have been corrected. Lines dropped from poems have been reinstated. The largest number of faults arose during the editing of the late, unpublished poetry which Crane had not, as was his custom, transcribed into final, typed form. Fortunately, the manuscripts survived and were available for scrutiny. A detailed accounting of all corrections, as well as of the documents upon which editorial judgments were based, is set forth in the notes at the rear of this book. It may be claimed modestly that the reader at last has a text of Hart Crane's poetry upon which he can rely for years to come.

The position of the glosses in *The Bridge* was of great importance to Crane. Because the size of the page in the paperback edition did not permit of placing them on the same page, I have adopted the expedient of putting them on the facing page (either right or left, as Crane indicated) so that the reader may see them exactly where Crane intended them to be. Although this arrangement results in a certain amount of blank space which did not appear in the original edition, it does give a greater fidelity to the original than was possible in the previous paperback edition.

I am indebted to Pyke Johnson for his sensitive willingness to sponsor a new edition of Crane's poems and to Samuel Loveman, David Mann, and Arthur Pell for authorizing it. The generosity of Columbia University Libraries in permitting me to print unpublished materials from the unique Hart Crane Collection, and to use the Special Manuscripts department freely for reference purposes, was essential for the proper preparation of this book; it was pleasing to a nostalgic ex-New Yorker and provides a model all libraries should emulate. I hastily add that the libraries of Yale University, Brown University, Ohio State University, Rutgers University, the University of Chicago, the University of Washington, and the University of California, Davis, were also helpful. In addition, I gratefully acknowledge that the Graduate School of the University of Minnesota and the Committee on Research of the Davis Division of the Academic Senate of the University of California provided me with funds to pay for much of the travel, clerical, and other expenses incurred during the preparation of this edition. For special favors granted I warmly thank Gerry Baker, Lynn Barry, Roland Baughman, Donald Gallup, David Ignatow, Marian Koritz, Lewis Leary, Kenneth Lohf, Norman Holmes Pearson, John Unterecker, and Mary Whouley.

BROM WEBER

ONE

White Buildings

TO WALDO FRANK ·

Ce ne peut être que la fin du monde, en avançant.
RIMBAUD

LEGEND

As silent as a mirror is believed
Realities plunge in silence by . . .

I am not ready for repentance;
Nor to match regrets. For the moth
Bends no more than the still
Imploring flame. And tremorous
In the white falling flakes
Kisses are,—
The only worth all granting.

It is to be learned—
This cleaving and this burning,
But only by the one who
Spends out himself again.

Twice and twice
(Again the smoking souvenir,
Bleeding eidolon!) and yet again.
Until the bright logic is won
Unwhispering as a mirror
Is believed.

Then, drop by caustic drop, a perfect cry
Shall string some constant harmony,—
Relentless caper for all those who step
The legend of their youth into the noon.

BLACK TAMBOURINE

The interests of a black man in a cellar
Mark tardy judgment on the world's closed door.
Gnats toss in the shadow of a bottle,
And a roach spans a crevice in the floor.

Æsop, driven to pondering, found
Heaven with the tortoise and the hare;
Fox brush and sow ear top his grave
And mingling incantations on the air.

The black man, forlorn in the cellar,
Wanders in some mid-kingdom, dark, that lies,
Between his tambourine, stuck on the wall,
And, in Africa, a carcass quick with flies.

EMBLEMS OF CONDUCT

By a peninsula the wanderer sat and sketched
The uneven valley graves. While the apostle gave
Alms to the meek the volcano burst
With sulphur and aureate rocks . . .
For joy rides in stupendous coverings
Luring the living into spiritual gates.

Orators follow the universe
And radio the complete laws to the people.
The apostle conveys thought through discipline.
Bowls and cups fill historians with adorations,—
Dull lips commemorating spiritual gates.

The wanderer later chose this spot of rest
Where marble clouds support the sea
And where was finally borne a chosen hero.
By that time summer and smoke were past.
Dolphins still played, arching the horizons,
But only to build memories of spiritual gates.

MY GRANDMOTHER'S LOVE LETTERS

There are no stars to-night
But those of memory.
Yet how much room for memory there is
In the loose girdle of soft rain.

There is even room enough
For the letters of my mother's mother,
Elizabeth,
That have been pressed so long
Into a corner of the roof
That they are brown and soft,
And liable to melt as snow.

Over the greatness of such space
Steps must be gentle.
It is all hung by an invisible white hair.
It trembles as birch limbs webbing the air.

And I ask myself:

"Are your fingers long enough to play
Old keys that are but echoes:
Is the silence strong enough
To carry back the music to its source
And back to you again
As though to her?"

Yet I would lead my grandmother by the hand
Through much of what she would not understand;
And so I stumble. And the rain continues on the roof
With such a sound of gently pitying laughter.

SUNDAY MORNING APPLES

To William Sommer

The leaves will fall again sometime and fill
The fleece of nature with those purposes
That are your rich and faithful strength of line.

But now there are challenges to spring
In that ripe nude with head
                         reared
Into a realm of swords, her purple shadow
Bursting on the winter of the world
From whiteness that cries defiance to the snow.

A boy runs with a dog before the sun, straddling
Spontaneities that form their independent orbits,
Their own perennials of light
In the valley where you live
                        (called Brandywine).

I have seen the apples there that toss you secrets,—
Beloved apples of seasonable madness
That feed your inquiries with aerial wine.

Put them again beside a pitcher with a knife,
And poise them full and ready for explosion—
The apples, Bill, the apples!

PRAISE FOR AN URN

In Memoriam: Ernest Nelson

It was a kind and northern face
That mingled in such exile guise
The everlasting eyes of Pierrot
And, of Gargantua, the laughter.

His thoughts, delivered to me
From the white coverlet and pillow,
I see now, were inheritances—
Delicate riders of the storm.

The slant moon on the slanting hill
Once moved us toward presentiments
Of what the dead keep, living still,
And such assessments of the soul

As, perched in the crematory lobby,
The insistent clock commented on,
Touching as well upon our praise
Of glories proper to the time.

Still, having in mind gold hair,
I cannot see that broken brow
And miss the dry sound of bees
Stretching across a lucid space.

Scatter these well-meant idioms
Into the smoky spring that fills
The suburbs, where they will be lost.
They are no trophies of the sun.

8

GARDEN ABSTRACT

The apple on its bough is her desire,—
Shining suspension, mimic of the sun.
The bough has caught her breath up, and her voice,
Dumbly articulate in the slant and rise
Of branch on branch above her, blurs her eyes.
She is prisoner of the tree and its green fingers.

And so she comes to dream herself the tree,
The wind possessing her, weaving her young veins,
Holding her to the sky and its quick blue,
Drowning the fever of her hands in sunlight.
She has no memory, nor fear, nor hope
Beyond the grass and shadows at her feet.

STARK MAJOR

The lover's death, how regular
With lifting spring and starker
Vestiges of the sun that somehow
Filter in to us before we waken.

Not yet is there that heat and sober
Vivisection of more clamant air
That hands joined in the dark will answer
After the daily circuits of its glare.

It is the time of sundering . . .
Beneath the green silk counterpane
Her mound of undelivered life
Lies cool upon her—not yet pain.

And she will wake before you pass,
Scarcely aloud, beyond her door,
And every third step down the stair
Until you reach the muffled floor—

Will laugh and call your name; while you
Still answering her faint good-byes,
Will find the street, only to look
At doors and stone with broken eyes.

Walk now, and note the lover's death.
Henceforth her memory is more
Than yours, in cries, in ecstasies
You cannot ever reach to share.

CHAPLINESQUE

We make our meek adjustments,
Contented with such random consolations
As the wind deposits
In slithered and too ample pockets.

For we can still love the world, who find
A famished kitten on the step, and know
Recesses for it from the fury of the street,
Or warm torn elbow coverts.

We will sidestep, and to the final smirk
Dally the doom of that inevitable thumb
That slowly chafes its puckered index toward us,
Facing the dull squint with what innocence
And what surprise!

And yet these fine collapses are not lies
More than the pirouettes of any pliant cane;
Our obsequies are, in a way, no enterprise.
We can evade you, and all else but the heart:
What blame to us if the heart live on.

The game enforces smirks; but we have seen
The moon in lonely alleys make
A grail of laughter of an empty ash can,
And through all sound of gaiety and quest
Have heard a kitten in the wilderness.

PASTORALE

No more violets,
And the year
Broken into smoky panels.
What woods remember now
Her calls, her enthusiasms.

That ritual of sap and leaves
The sun drew out,
Ends in this latter muffled
Bronze and brass. The wind
Takes rein.

If, dusty, I bear
An image beyond this
Already fallen harvest,
I can only query, "Fool—
Have you remembered too long;

Or was there too little said
For ease or resolution—
Summer scarcely begun
And violets,
A few picked, the rest dead?"

IN SHADOW

Out in the late amber afternoon,
Confused among chrysanthemums,
Her parasol, a pale balloon,
Like a waiting moon, in shadow swims.

Her furtive lace and misty hair
Over the garden dial distill
The sunlight,—then withdrawing, wear
Again the shadows at her will.

Gently yet suddenly, the sheen
Of stars inwraps her parasol.
She hears my step behind the green
Twilight, stiller than shadows, fall.

"Come, it is too late,—too late
To risk alone the light's decline:
Nor has the evening long to wait,"—
But her own words are night's and mine.

THE FERNERY

The lights that travel on her spectacles
Seldom, now, meet a mirror in her eyes.
But turning, as you may chance to lift a shade
Beside her and her fernery, is to follow
The zigzags fast around dry lips composed
To darkness through a wreath of sudden pain.

—So, while fresh sunlight splinters humid green
I have known myself a nephew to confusions
That sometimes take up residence and reign
In crowns less grey—O merciless tidy hair!

NORTH LABRADOR

A land of leaning ice
Hugged by plaster-grey arches of sky,
Flings itself silently
Into eternity.

"Has no one come here to win you,
Or left you with the faintest blush
Upon your glittering breasts?
Have you no memories, O Darkly Bright?"

Cold-hushed, there is only the shifting of moments
That journey toward no Spring—
No birth, no death, no time nor sun
In answer.

REPOSE OF RIVERS

The willows carried a slow sound,
A sarabande the wind mowed on the mead.
I could never remember
That seething, steady leveling of the marshes
Till age had brought me to the sea.

Flags, weeds. And remembrance of steep alcoves
Where cypresses shared the noon's
Tyranny; they drew me into hades almost.
And mammoth turtles climbing sulphur dreams
Yielded, while sun-silt rippled them
Asunder . . .

How much I would have bartered! the black gorge
And all the singular nestings in the hills
Where beavers learn stitch and tooth.
The pond I entered once and quickly fled—
I remember now its singing willow rim.

And finally, in that memory all things nurse;
After the city that I finally passed
With scalding unguents spread and smoking darts
The monsoon cut across the delta
At gulf gates . . . There, beyond the dykes

I heard wind flaking sapphire, like this summer,
And willows could not hold more steady sound.

PARAPHRASE

Of a steady winking beat between
Systole, diastole spokes-of-a-wheel
One rushing from the bed at night
May find the record wedged in his soul.

Above the feet the clever sheets
Lie guard upon the integers of life:
For what skims in between uncurls the toe,
Involves the hands in purposeless repose.

But from its bracket how can the tongue tell
When systematic morn shall sometime flood
The pillow—how desperate is the light
That shall not rouse, how faint the crow's cavil

As, when stunned in that antarctic blaze,
Your head, unrocking to a pulse, already
Hollowed by air, posts a white paraphrase
Among bruised roses on the papered wall.

POSSESSIONS

Witness now this trust! the rain
That steals softly direction
And the key, ready to hand—sifting
One moment in sacrifice (the direst)
Through a thousand nights the flesh
Assaults outright for bolts that linger
Hidden,—O undirected as the sky
That through its black foam has no eyes
For this fixed stone of lust . . .

Accumulate such moments to an hour:
Account the total of this trembling tabulation.
I know the screen, the distant flying taps
And stabbing medley that sways—
And the mercy, feminine, that stays
As though prepared.

And I, entering, take up the stone
As quiet as you can make a man . . .
In Bleecker Street, still trenchant in a void,
Wounded by apprehensions out of speech,
I hold it up against a disk of light—
I, turning, turning on smoked forking spires,
The city's stubborn lives, desires.

Tossed on these horns, who bleeding dies,
Lacks all but piteous admissions to be spilt
Upon the page whose blind sum finally burns
Record of rage and partial appetites.
The pure possession, the inclusive cloud
Whose heart is fire shall come,—the white wind rase
All but bright stones wherein our smiling plays.

LACHRYMAE CHRISTI

Whitely, while benzine
Rinsings from the moon
Dissolve all but the windows of the mills
(Inside the sure machinery
Is still
And curdled only where a sill
Sluices its one unyielding smile)

Immaculate venom binds
The fox's teeth, and swart
Thorns freshen on the year's
First blood. From flanks untended,
Twanged red perfidies of spring
Are trillion on the hill.

And the nights opening
Chant pyramids,—
Anoint with innocence,—recall
To music and retrieve what perjuries
Had galvanized the eyes.

             While chime
Beneath and all around
Distilling clemencies,—worms'
Inaudible whistle, tunneling
Not penitence
But song, as these
Perpetual fountains, vines,—

Thy Nazarene and tinder eyes.

(Let sphinxes from the ripe
Borage of death have cleared my tongue
Once and again; vermin and rod
No longer bind. Some sentient cloud
Of tears flocks through the tendoned loam:
Betrayed stones slowly speak.)

Names peeling from Thine eyes
And their undimming lattices of flame,
Spell out in palm and pain
Compulsion of the year, O Nazarene.

Lean long from sable, slender boughs,
Unstanched and luminous. And as the nights
Strike from Thee perfect spheres,
Lift up in lilac-emerald breath the grail
Of earth again—

                    Thy face
From charred and riven stakes, O
Dionysus, Thy
Unmangled target smile.

PASSAGE

Where the cedar leaf divides the sky
I heard the sea.
In sapphire arenas of the hills
I was promised an improved infancy.

Sulking, sanctioning the sun,
My memory I left in a ravine,—
Casual louse that tissues the buckwheat,
Aprons rocks, congregates pears
In moonlit bushels
And wakens alleys with a hidden cough.

Dangerously the summer burned
(I had joined the entrainments of the wind).
The shadows of boulders lengthened my back:
In the bronze gongs of my cheeks
The rain dried without odour.

"It is not long, it is not long;
See where the red and black
Vine-stanchioned valleys—": but the wind
Died speaking through the ages that you know
And hug, chimney-sooted heart of man!
So was I turned about and back, much as your smoke
Compiles a too well-known biography.

The evening was a spear, in the ravine
That throve through very oak. And had I walked
The dozen particular decimals of time?
Touching an opening laurel, I found
A thief beneath, my stolen book in hand.

"Why are you back here—smiling an iron coffin?"
"To argue with the laurel," I replied:
"Am justified in transience, fleeing
Under the constant wonder of your eyes—."

He closed the book. And from the Ptolemies
Sand troughed us in a glittering abyss.
A serpent swam a vertex to the sun
—On unpaced beaches leaned its tongue and
    drummed.
What fountains did I hear? what icy speeches?
Memory, committed to the page, had broke.

THE WINE MENAGERIE

Invariably when wine redeems the sight,
Narrowing the mustard scansions of the eyes,
A leopard ranging always in the brow
Asserts a vision in the slumbering gaze.

Then glozening decanters that reflect the street
Wear me in crescents on their bellies. Slow
Applause flows into liquid cynosures:
—I am conscripted to their shadows' glow.

Against the imitation onyx wainscoting
(Painted emulsion of snow, eggs, yarn, coal, manure)
Regard the forceps of the smile that takes her.
Percussive sweat is spreading to his hair. Mallets,
Her eyes, unmake an instant of the world . . .

What is it in this heap the serpent pries—
Whose skin, facsimile of time, unskeins
Octagon, sapphire transepts round the eyes;
—From whom some whispered carillon assures
Speed to the arrow into feathered skies?

Sharp to the windowpane guile drags a face,
And as the alcove of her jealousy recedes
An urchin who has left the snow
Nudges a cannister across the bar
While August meadows somewhere clasp his brow.

Each chamber, transept, coins some squint,
Remorseless line, minting their separate wills—
Poor streaked bodies wreathing up and out,
Unwitting the stigma that each turn repeals:
Between black tusks the roses shine!

New thresholds, new anatomies! Wine talons
Build freedom up about me and distill
This competence—to travel in a tear
Sparkling alone, within another's will.

Until my blood dreams a receptive smile
Wherein new purities are snared; where chimes
Before some flame of gaunt repose a shell
Tolled once, perhaps, by every tongue in hell.
—Anguished, the wit that cries out of me:

"Alas,—these frozen billows of your skill!
Invent new dominoes of love and bile . . .
Ruddy, the tooth implicit of the world
Has followed you. Though in the end you know
And count some dim inheritance of sand,
How much yet meets the treason of the snow.

"Rise from the dates and crumbs. And walk away,
Stepping over Holofernes' shins—
Beyond the wall, whose severed head floats by
With Baptist John's. Their whispering begins.

"—And fold your exile on your back again;
Petrushka's valentine pivots on its pin."

24

RECITATIVE

Regard the capture here, O Janus-faced,
As double as the hands that twist this glass.
Such eyes at search or rest you cannot see;
Reciting pain or glee, how can you bear!

Twin shadowed halves: the breaking second holds
In each the skin alone, and so it is
I crust a plate of vibrant mercury
Borne cleft to you, and brother in the half.

Inquire this much-exacting fragment smile,
Its drums and darkest blowing leaves ignore,—
Defer though, revocation of the tears
That yield attendance to one crucial sign.

Look steadily—how the wind feasts and spins
The brain's disk shivered against lust. Then watch
While darkness, like an ape's face, falls away,
And gradually white buildings answer day.

Let the same nameless gulf beleaguer us—
Alike suspend us from atrocious sums
Built floor by floor on shafts of steel that grant
The plummet heart, like Absalom, no stream.

The highest tower,—let her ribs palisade
Wrenched gold of Nineveh;—yet leave the tower.
The bridge swings over salvage, beyond wharves;
A wind abides the ensign of your will . . .

In alternating bells have you not heard
All hours clapped dense into a single stride?
Forgive me for an echo of these things,
And let us walk through time with equal pride.

FOR THE MARRIAGE OF FAUSTUS
AND HELEN

"And so we may arrive by Talmud skill
And profane Greek to raise the building up
Of Helen's house against the Ismaelite,
King of Thogarma, and his habergeons
Brimstony, blue and fiery; and the force
Of King Abaddon, and the beast of Cittim;
Which Rabbi David Kimchi, Onkelos,
And Aben Ezra do interpret Rome."
                                        THE ALCHEMIST

I

The mind has shown itself at times
Too much the baked and labeled dough
Divided by accepted multitudes.
Across the stacked partitions of the day—
Across the memoranda, baseball scores,
The stenographic smiles and stock quotations
Smutty wings flash out equivocations.

The mind is brushed by sparrow wings;
Numbers, rebuffed by asphalt, crowd
The margins of the day, accent the curbs,
Convoying divers dawns on every corner
To druggist, barber and tobacconist,
Until the graduate opacities of evening
Take them away as suddenly to somewhere
Virginal perhaps, less fragmentary, cool.

27

> *There is the world dimensional for*
> *those untwisted by the love of things*
> *irreconcilable . . .*

And yet, suppose some evening I forgot
The fare and transfer, yet got by that way
Without recall,—lost yet poised in traffic.
Then I might find your eyes across an aisle,
Still flickering with those prefigurations—
Prodigal, yet uncontested now,
Half-riant before the jerky window frame.

There is some way, I think, to touch
Those hands of yours that count the nights
Stippled with pink and green advertisements.
And now, before its arteries turn dark
I would have you meet this bartered blood.
Imminent in his dream, none better knows
The white wafer cheek of love, or offers words
Lightly as moonlight on the eaves meets snow.

Reflective conversion of all things
At your deep blush, when ecstasies thread
The limbs and belly, when rainbows spread
Impinging on the throat and sides . . .
Inevitable, the body of the world
Weeps in inventive dust for the hiatus
That winks above it, bluet in your breasts.

The earth may glide diaphanous to death;
But if I lift my arms it is to bend
To you who turned away once, Helen, knowing
The press of troubled hands, too alternate
With steel and soil to hold you endlessly.
I meet you, therefore, in that eventual flame

You found in final chains, no captive then—
Beyond their million brittle, bloodshot eyes;
White, through white cities passed on to assume
That world which comes to each of us alone.

Accept a lone eye riveted to your plane,
Bent axle of devotion along companion ways
That beat, continuous, to hourless days—
One inconspicuous, glowing orb of praise.

II

Brazen hynotics glitter here;
Glee shifts from foot to foot,
Magnetic to their tremolo.
This crashing opéra bouffe,
Blest excursion! this ricochet
From roof to roof—
Know, Olympians, we are breathless
While nigger cupids scour the stars!

A thousand light shrugs balance us
Through snarling hails of melody.
White shadows slip across the floor
Splayed like cards from a loose hand;
Rhythmic ellipses lead into canters
Until somewhere a rooster banters.

Greet naïvely—yet intrepidly
New soothings, new amazements
That cornets introduce at every turn—
And you may fall downstairs with me
With perfect grace and equanimity.
Or, plaintively scud past shores
Where, by strange harmonic laws
All relatives, serene and cool,
Sit rocked in patent armchairs.

O, I have known metallic paradises
Where cuckoos clucked to finches
Above the deft catastrophes of drums.
While titters hailed the groans of death

Beneath gyrating awnings I have seen
The incunabula of the divine grotesque.
This music has a reassuring way.

The siren of the springs of guilty song—
Let us take her on the incandescent wax
Striated with nuances, nervosities
That we are heir to: she is still so young,
We cannot frown upon her as she smiles,
Dipping here in this cultivated storm
Among slim skaters of the gardened skies.

III

Capped arbiter of beauty in this street
That narrows darkly into motor dawn,—
You, here beside me, delicate ambassador
Of intricate slain numbers that arise
In whispers, naked of steel;

       religious gunman!
Who faithfully, yourself, will fall too soon,
And in other ways than as the wind settles
On the sixteen thrifty bridges of the city:
Let us unbind our throats of fear and pity.

      We even,
Who drove speediest destruction
In corymbulous formations of mechanics,—
Who hurried the hill breezes, spouting malice
Plangent over meadows, and looked down
On rifts of torn and empty houses
Like old women with teeth unjubilant
That waited faintly, briefly and in vain:

We know, eternal gunman, our flesh remembers
The tensile boughs, the nimble blue plateaus,
The mounted, yielding cities of the air!

That saddled sky that shook down vertical
Repeated play of fire—no hypogeum
Of wave or rock was good against one hour.

We did not ask for that, but have survived,
And will persist to speak again before
All stubble streets that have not curved
To memory, or known the ominous lifted arm
That lowers down the arc of Helen's brow
To saturate with blessing and dismay.

A goose, tobacco and cologne—
Three-winged and gold-shod prophecies of heaven,
The lavish heart shall always have to leaven
And spread with bells and voices, and atone
The abating shadows of our conscript dust.

Anchises' navel, dripping of the sea,—
The hands Erasmus dipped in gleaming tides,
Gathered the voltage of blown blood and vine;
Delve upward for the new and scattered wine,
O brother-thief of time, that we recall.
Laugh out the meager penance of their days
Who dare not share with us the breath released,
The substance drilled and spent beyond repair
For golden, or the shadow of gold hair.

Distinctly praise the years, whose volatile
Blamed bleeding hands extend and thresh the height
The imagination spans beyond despair,
Outpacing bargain, vocable and prayer.

AT MELVILLE'S TOMB

Often beneath the wave, wide from this ledge
The dice of drowned men's bones he saw bequeath
An embassy. Their numbers as he watched,
Beat on the dusty shore and were obscured.

And wrecks passed without sound of bells,
The calyx of death's bounty giving back
A scattered chapter, livid hieroglyph,
The portent wound in corridors of shells.

Then in the circuit calm of one vast coil,
Its lashings charmed and malice reconciled,
Frosted eyes there were that lifted altars;
And silent answers crept across the stars.

Compass, quadrant and sextant contrive
No farther tides . . . High in the azure steeps
Monody shall not wake the mariner.
This fabulous shadow only the sea keeps.

VOYAGES

I

Above the fresh ruffles of the surf
Bright striped urchins flay each other with sand.
They have contrived a conquest for shell shucks,
And their fingers crumble fragments of baked weed
Gaily digging and scattering.

And in answer to their treble interjections
The sun beats lightning on the waves,
The waves fold thunder on the sand;
And could they hear me I would tell them:

O brilliant kids, frisk with your dog,
Fondle your shells and sticks, bleached
By time and the elements; but there is a line
You must not cross nor ever trust beyond it
Spry cordage of your bodies to caresses
Too lichen-faithful from too wide a breast.
The bottom of the sea is cruel.

II

—And yet this great wink of eternity,
Of rimless floods, unfettered leewardings,
Samite sheeted and processioned where
Her undinal vast belly moonward bends,
Laughing the wrapt inflections of our love;

Take this Sea, whose diapason knells
On scrolls of silver snowy sentences,
The sceptred terror of whose sessions rends
As her demeanors motion well or ill,
All but the pieties of lovers' hands.

And onward, as bells off San Salvador
Salute the crocus lustres of the stars,
In these poinsettia meadows of her tides,—
Adagios of islands, O my Prodigal,
Complete the dark confessions her veins spell.

Mark how her turning shoulders wind the hours,
And hasten while her penniless rich palms
Pass superscription of bent foam and wave,—
Hasten, while they are true,—sleep, death, desire,
Close round one instant in one floating flower.

Bind us in time, O Seasons clear, and awe.
O minstrel galleons of Carib fire,
Bequeath us to no earthly shore until
Is answered in the vortex of our grave
The seal's wide spindrift gaze toward paradise.

III

Infinite consanguinity it bears—
This tendered theme of you that light
Retrieves from sea plains where the sky
Resigns a breast that every wave enthrones;
While ribboned water lanes I wind
Are laved and scattered with no stroke
Wide from your side, whereto this hour
The sea lifts, also, reliquary hands.

And so, admitted through black swollen gates
That must arrest all distance otherwise,—
Past whirling pillars and lithe pediments,
Light wrestling there incessantly with light,
Star kissing star through wave on wave unto
Your body rocking!
        and where death, if shed,
Presumes no carnage, but this single change,—
Upon the steep floor flung from dawn to dawn
The silken skilled transmemberment of song;

Permit me voyage, love, into your hands . . .

IV

Whose counted smile of hours and days, suppose
I know as spectrum of the sea and pledge
Vastly now parting gulf on gulf of wings
Whose circles bridge, I know, (from palms to the
    severe
Chilled albatross's white immutability)
No stream of greater love advancing now
Than, singing, this mortality alone
Through clay aflow immortally to you.

All fragrance irrefragibly, and claim
Madly meeting logically in this hour
And region that is ours to wreathe again,
Portending eyes and lips and making told
The chancel port and portion of our June—

Shall they not stem and close in our own steps
Bright staves of flowers and quills to-day as I
Must first be lost in fatal tides to tell?

In signature of the incarnate word
The harbor shoulders to resign in mingling
Mutual blood, transpiring as foreknown
And widening noon within your breast for gathering
All bright insinuations that my years have caught
For islands where must lead inviolably
Blue latitudes and levels of your eyes,—

In this expectant, still exclaim receive
The secret oar and petals of all love.

V.

Meticulous, past midnight in clear rime,
Infrangible and lonely, smooth as though cast
Together in one merciless white blade—
The bay estuaries fleck the hard sky limits.

—As if too brittle or too clear to touch!
The cables of our sleep so swiftly filed,
Already hang, shred ends from remembered stars.
One frozen trackless smile . . . What words
Can strangle this deaf moonlight? For we

Are overtaken. Now no cry, no sword
Can fasten or deflect this tidal wedge,
Slow tyranny of moonlight, moonlight loved
And changed . . . "There's

Nothing like this in the world," you say,
Knowing I cannot touch your hand and look
Too, into that godless cleft of sky
Where nothing turns but dead sands flashing.

"—And never to quite understand!" No,
In all the argosy of your bright hair I dreamed
Nothing so flagless as this piracy.

                              But now
Draw in your head, alone and too tall here.
Your eyes already in the slant of drifting foam;
Your breath sealed by the ghosts I do not know:
Draw in your head and sleep the long way home.

VI

Where icy and bright dungeons lift
Of swimmers their lost morning eyes,
And ocean rivers, churning, shift
Green borders under stranger skies,

Steadily as a shell secretes
Its beating leagues of monotone,
Or as many waters trough the sun's
Red kelson past the cape's wet stone;

O rivers mingling toward the sky
And harbor of the phœnix' breast—
My eyes pressed black against the prow,
—Thy derelict and blinded guest

Waiting, afire, what name, unspoke,
I cannot claim: let thy waves rear
More savage than the death of kings,
Some splintered garland for the seer.

Beyond siroccos harvesting
The solstice thunders, crept away,
Like a cliff swinging or a sail
Flung into April's inmost day—

Creation's blithe and petalled word
To the lounged goddess when she rose
Conceding dialogue with eyes
That smile unsearchable repose—

Still fervid covenant, Belle Isle,
—Unfolded floating dais before
Which rainbows twine continual hair—
Belle Isle, white echo of the oar!

The imaged Word, it is, that holds
Hushed willows anchored in its glow.
It is the unbetrayable reply
Whose accent no farewell can know.

TWO

The Bridge

From going to and fro in the earth,
and from walking up and down in it.
THE BOOK OF JOB

To Brooklyn Bridge

How many dawns, chill from his rippling rest
The seagull's wings shall dip and pivot him,
Shedding white rings of tumult, building high
Over the chained bay waters Liberty—

Then, with inviolate curve, forsake our eyes
As apparitional as sails that cross
Some page of figures to be filed away;
—Till elevators drop us from our day . . .

I think of cinemas, panoramic sleights
With multitudes bent toward some flashing scene
Never disclosed, but hastened to again,
Foretold to other eyes on the same screen;

And Thee, across the harbor, silver-paced
As though the sun took step of thee, yet left
Some motion ever unspent in thy stride,—
Implicitly thy freedom staying thee!

Out of some subway scuttle, cell or loft
A bedlamite speeds to thy parapets,
Tilting there momently, shrill shirt ballooning,
A jest falls from the speechless caravan.

Down Wall, from girder into street noon leaks,
A rip-tooth of the sky's acetylene;
All afternoon the cloud-flown derricks turn . . .
Thy cables breathe the North Atlantic still.

And obscure as that heaven of the Jews,
Thy guerdon . . . Accolade thou dost bestow
Of anonymity time cannot raise:
Vibrant reprieve and pardon thou dost show.

O harp and altar, of the fury fused,
(How could mere toil align thy choiring strings!)
Terrific threshold of the prophet's pledge,
Prayer of pariah, and the lover's cry,—

Again the traffic lights that skim thy swift
Unfractioned idiom, immaculate sigh of stars,
Beading thy path—condense eternity:
And we have seen night lifted in thine arms.

Under thy shadow by the piers I waited;
Only in darkness is thy shadow clear.
The City's fiery parcels all undone,
Already snow submerges an iron year . . .

O Sleepless as the river under thee,
Vaulting the sea, the prairies' dreaming sod,
Unto us lowliest sometime sweep, descend
And of the curveship lend a myth to God.

I

Ave Maria

> *Venient annis, sæcula seris,*
> *Quibus Oceanus vincula rerum*
> *Laxet et ingens pateat tellus*
> *Tiphysque novos detegat orbes*
> *Nec sit terris ultima Thule.*
> **SENECA**

Be with me, Luis de San Angel, now—
Witness before the tides can wrest away
The word I bring, O you who reined my suit
Into the Queen's great heart that doubtful day;
For I have seen now what no perjured breath
Of clown nor sage can riddle or gainsay;—
To you, too, Juan Perez, whose counsel fear
And greed adjourned,—I bring you back Cathay!

Here waves climb into dusk on gleaming mail;
Invisible valves of the sea,—locks, tendons
Crested and creeping, troughing corridors
That fall back yawning to another plunge.
Slowly the sun's red caravel drops light
Once more behind us. . . . It is morning there—
O where our Indian emperies lie revealed,
Yet lost, all, let this keel one instant yield!

I thought of Genoa; and this truth, now proved,
That made me exile in her streets, stood me
More absolute than ever—biding the moon
Till dawn should clear that dim frontier, first seen
—The Chan's great continent. . . . Then faith, not
      fear
Nigh surged me witless. . . . Hearing the surf near—
I, wonder-breathing, kept the watch,—saw
The first palm chevron the first lighted hill.

And lowered. And they came out to us crying,
"The Great White Birds!" (O Madre María, still
One ship of these thou grantest safe returning;
Assure us through thy mantle's ageless blue!)

48

*Columbus,
alone, gazing
toward Spain,
invokes the
presence of
two faithful
partisans of
his quest . . .*

And record of more, floating in a casque,
Was tumbled from us under bare poles scudding;
And later hurricanes may claim more pawn. . . .
For here between two worlds, another, harsh,

This third, of water, tests the word; lo, here
Bewilderment and mutiny heap whelming
Laughter, and shadow cuts sleep from the heart
Almost as though the Moor's flung scimitar
Found more than flesh to fathom in its fall.
Yet under tempest-lash and surfeitings
Some inmost sob, half-heard, dissuades the abyss,
Merges the wind in measure to the waves,

Series on series, infinite,—till eyes
Starved wide on blackened tides, accrete—enclose
This turning rondure whole, this crescent ring
Sun-cusped and zoned with modulated fire
Like pearls that whisper through the Doge's hands
—Yet no delirium of jewels! O Fernando,
Take of that eastern shore, this western sea,
Yet yield thy God's, thy Virgin's charity!

—Rush down the plenitude, and you shall see
Isaiah counting famine on this lee!

* * *

An herb, a stray branch among salty teeth,
The jellied weeds that drag the shore,—perhaps
Tomorrow's moon will grant us Saltes Bar—
Palos again,—a land cleared of long war.
Some Angelus environs the cordage tree;
Dark waters onward shake the dark prow free.

* * *

O Thou who sleepest on Thyself, apart
Like ocean athwart lanes of death and birth,
And all the eddying breath between dost search
Cruelly with love thy parable of man,—
Inquisitor! incognizable Word
Of Eden and the enchained Sepulchre,
Into thy steep savannahs, burning blue,
Utter to loneliness the sail is true.

Who grindest oar, and arguing the mast
Subscribest holocaust of ships, O Thou
Within whose primal scan consummately
The glistening seignories of Ganges swim;—
Who sendest greeting by the corposant,
And Teneriffe's garnet—flamed it in a cloud,
Urging through night our passage to the Chan;—
Te Deum laudamus, for thy teeming span!

Of all that amplitude that time explores,
A needle in the sight, suspended north,—
Yielding by inference and discard, faith
And true appointment from the hidden shoal:
This disposition that thy night relates
From Moon to Saturn in one sapphire wheel:
The orbic wake of thy once whirling feet,
Elohim, still I hear thy sounding heel!

White toil of heaven's cordons, mustering
In holy rings all sails charged to the far
Hushed gleaming fields and pendant seething wheat
Of knowledge,—round thy brows unhooded now
—The kindled Crown! acceded of the poles
And biassed by full sails, meridians reel
Thy purpose—still one shore beyond desire!
The sea's green crying towers a-sway, Beyond

And kingdoms
       naked in the
              trembling heart—
Te Deum laudamus
              O Thou Hand of Fire

II

Powhatan's Daughter

> "—Pocahuntus, a well-featured but wanton yong girle . . . of the age of eleven or twelve years, get the boyes forth with her into the market place, and make them wheele, falling on their hands, turning their heels upwards, whom she would followe, and wheele so herself, naked as she was, all the fort over."

THE HARBOR DAWN

Insistently through sleep—a tide of voices—
They meet you listening midway in your dream,
The long, tired sounds, fog-insulated noises:
Gongs in white surplices, beshrouded wails,
Far strum of fog horns . . . signals dispersed in veils.

And then a truck will lumber past the wharves
As winch engines begin throbbing on some deck;
Or a drunken stevedore's howl and thud below
Comes echoing alley-upward through dim snow.

And if they take your sleep away sometimes
They give it back again. Soft sleeves of sound
Attend the darkling harbor, the pillowed bay;
Somewhere out there in blankness steam

Spills into steam, and wanders, washed away
—Flurried by keen fifings, eddied
Among distant chiming buoys—adrift. The sky,
Cool feathery fold, suspends, distills
This wavering slumber. . . . Slowly—
Immemorially the window, the half-covered chair
Ask nothing but this sheath of pallid air.

And you beside me, blessèd now while sirens
Sing to us, stealthily weave us into day—
Serenely now, before day claims our eyes
Your cool arms murmurously about me lay.

While myriad snowy hands are clustering at the
    panes—

*400 years and
more . . . or is
it from the
soundless shore
of sleep that
time*

*recalls you to
your love,
there in a
waking dream
to merge
your seed*

your hands within my hands are deeds;
my tongue upon your throat—singing
arms close; eyes wide, undoubtful
                    dark
                              drink the dawn—
a forest shudders in your hair!

The window goes blond slowly. Frostily clears.
From Cyclopean towers across Manhattan waters
—Two—three bright window-eyes aglitter, disk
The sun, released—aloft with cold gulls hither.

The fog leans one last moment on the sill.
Under the mistletoe of dreams, a star—
As though to join us at some distant hill—
Turns in the waking west and goes to sleep.

—with whom?

*Who is the
woman with
us in the
dawn? . . .
whose is the
flesh our feet
have moved
upon?*

VAN WINKLE

Macadam, gun-grey as the tunny's belt,
Leaps from Far Rockaway to Golden Gate:
Listen! the miles a hurdy-gurdy grinds—
Down gold arpeggios mile on mile unwinds.

Times earlier, when you hurried off to school,
—It is the same hour though a later day—
You walked with Pizarro in a copybook,
And Cortes rode up, reining tautly in—
Firmly as coffee grips the taste,—and away!

There was Priscilla's cheek close in the wind,
And Captain Smith, all beard and certainty,
And Rip Van Winkle bowing by the way,—
"Is this Sleepy Hollow, friend—?" And he—

And Rip forgot the office hours,
                    and he forgot the pay;
        Van Winkle sweeps a tenement
                            way down on Avenue A,—

*Streets spread
past store and
factory—sped
by sunlight
and her
smile . . .*

*Like Memory,
she is time's
truant, shall
take you by
the hand . . .*

The grind-organ says . . . Remember, remember
The cinder pile at the end of the backyard
Where we stoned the family of young
Garter snakes under . . . And the monoplanes
We launched—with paper wings and twisted
Rubber bands . . . Recall—recall

                                        the rapid tongues
That flittered from under the ash heap day
After day whenever your stick discovered
Some sunning inch of unsuspecting fibre—
It flashed back at your thrust, as clean as fire.

And Rip was slowly made aware
          that he, Van Winkle, was not here
   nor there. He woke and swore he'd seen Broadway
          a Catskill daisy chain in May—

So memory, that strikes a rhyme out of a box,
Or splits a random smell of flowers through glass—
Is it the whip stripped from the lilac tree
One day in spring my father took to me,
Or is it the Sabbatical, unconscious smile
My mother almost brought me once from church
And once only, as I recall—?

It flickered through the snow screen, blindly
It forsook her at the doorway, it was gone
Before I had left the window. It
Did not return with the kiss in the hall.

Macadam, gun-grey as the tunny's belt,
Leaps from Far Rockaway to Golden Gate. . . .
Keep hold of that nickel for car-change, Rip,—
Have you got your *"Times"*—?
And hurry along, Van Winkle—it's getting late!

THE RIVER

Stick your patent name on a signboard
brother—all over—going west—young man
Tintex—Japalac—Certain-teed Overalls ads
and lands sakes! under the new playbill ripped
in the guaranteed corner—see Bert Williams what?
Minstrels when you steal a chicken just
save me the wing for if it isn't
Erie it ain't for miles around a
Mazda—and the telegraphic night coming on Thomas

a Ediford—and whistling down the tracks
a headlight rushing with the sound—can you
imagine—while an EXPRESS makes time like
SCIENCE—COMMERCE and the HOLYGHOST
RADIO ROARS IN EVERY HOME WE HAVE THE NORTHPOLE
WALLSTREET AND VIRGINBIRTH WITHOUT STONES OR
WIRES OR EVEN RUNning brooks connecting ears
and no more sermons windows flashing roar
breathtaking—as you like it . . . eh?

　　　　So the 20th Century—so
whizzed the Limited—roared by and left
three men, still hungry on the tracks, ploddingly
watching the tail lights wizen and converge, slipping gimleted and neatly out of sight.

*　　　*　　　*

. . . and past
the din and
slogans of
the year—

The last bear, shot drinking in the Dakotas
Loped under wires that span the mountain stream.
Keen instruments, strung to a vast precision
Bind town to town and dream to ticking dream.
But some men take their liquor slow—and count
—Though they'll confess no rosary nor clue—
The river's minute by the far brook's year.
Under a world of whistles, wires and steam
Caboose-like they go ruminating through
Ohio, Indiana—blind baggage—
To Cheyenne tagging . . . Maybe Kalamazoo.

Time's rendings, time's blendings they construe
As final reckonings of fire and snow;
Strange bird-wit, like the elemental gist
Of unwalled winds they offer, singing low
My Old Kentucky Home and *Casey Jones*,
Some Sunny Day. I heard a road-gang chanting so.
And afterwards, who had a colt's eyes—one said,
"Jesus! Oh I remember watermelon days!" And sped
High in a cloud of merriment, recalled
"—And when my Aunt Sally Simpson smiled," he
          drawled—
"It was almost Louisiana, long ago."
"There's no place like Booneville though, Buddy,"
One said, excising a last burr from his vest,
"—For early trouting." Then peering in the can,
"—But I kept on the tracks." Possessed, resigned,
He trod the fire down pensively and grinned,
Spreading dry shingles of a beard. . . .

                              Behind
My father's cannery works I used to see
Rail-squatters ranged in nomad raillery,
The ancient men—wifeless or runaway
Hobo-trekkers that forever search
An empire wilderness of freight and rails.

Each seemed a child, like me, on a loose perch,
Holding to childhood like some termless play.
John, Jake or Charley, hopping the slow freight
—Memphis to Tallahassee—riding the rods,
Blind fists of nothing, humpty-dumpty clods.

Yet they touch something like a key perhaps.
From pole to pole across the hills, the states
—They know a body under the wide rain;
Youngsters with eyes like fjords, old reprobates
With racetrack jargon,—dotting immensity
They lurk across her, knowing her yonder breast
Snow-silvered, sumac-stained or smoky blue—
Is past the valley-sleepers, south or west.
—As I have trod the rumorous midnights, too,

And past the circuit of the lamp's thin flame
(O Nights that brought me to her body bare!)
Have dreamed beyond the print that bound her name.
Trains sounding the long blizzards out—I heard
Wail into distances I knew were hers.
Papooses crying on the wind's long mane
Screamed redskin dynasties that fled the brain,
—Dead echoes! But I knew her body there,
Time like a serpent down her shoulder, dark,
And space, an eaglet's wing, laid on her hair.

Under the Ozarks, domed by Iron Mountain,
The old gods of the rain lie wrapped in pools
Where eyeless fish curvet a sunken fountain
And re-descend with corn from querulous crows.
Such pilferings make up their timeless eatage,
Propitiate them for their timber torn
By iron, iron—always the iron dealt cleavage!
They doze now, below axe and powder horn.

66

but who have
touched her,
knowing her
without name

nor the
myths of her
fathers . . .

67

And Pullman breakfasters glide glistening steel
From tunnel into field—iron strides the dew—
Straddles the hill, a dance of wheel on wheel.
You have a half-hour's wait at Siskiyou,
Or stay the night and take the next train through.
Southward, near Cairo passing, you can see
The Ohio merging,—borne down Tennessee;
And if it's summer and the sun's in dusk
Maybe the breeze will lift the River's musk
—As though the waters breathed that you might know
Memphis Johnny, Steamboat Bill, Missouri Joe.
Oh, lean from the window, if the train slows down,
As though you touched hands with some ancient
    clown,
—A little while gaze absently below
And hum *Deep River* with them while they go.

Yes, turn again and sniff once more—look see,
O Sheriff, Brakeman and Authority—
Hitch up your pants and crunch another quid,
For you, too, feed the River timelessly.
And few evade full measure of their fate;
Always they smile out eerily what they seem.
I could believe he joked at heaven's gate—
Dan Midland—jolted from the cold brake-beam.

Down, down—born pioneers in time's despite,
Grimed tributaries to an ancient flow—
They win no frontier by their wayward plight,
But drift in stillness, as from Jordan's brow.

You will not hear it as the sea; even stone
Is not more hushed by gravity . . . But slow,
As loth to take more tribute—sliding prone
Like one whose eyes were buried long ago

The River, spreading, flows—and spends your dream.
What are you, lost within this tideless spell?
You are your father's father, and the stream—
A liquid theme that floating niggers swell.

Damp tonnage and alluvial march of days—
Nights turbid, vascular with silted shale
And roots surrendered down of moraine clays:
The Mississippi drinks the farthest dale.

O quarrying passion, undertowed sunlight!
The basalt surface drags a jungle grace
Ochreous and lynx-barred in lengthening might;
Patience! and you shall reach the biding place!

Over De Soto's bones the freighted floors
Throb past the City storied of three thrones.
Down two more turns the Mississippi pours
(Anon tall ironsides up from salt lagoons)

And flows within itself, heaps itself free.
All fades but one thin skyline 'round . . . Ahead
No embrace opens but the stinging sea;
The River lifts itself from its long bed,

Poised wholly on its dream, a mustard glow
Tortured with history, its one will—flow!
—The Passion spreads in wide tongues, choked and
    slow,
Meeting the Gulf, hosannas silently below.

THE DANCE

The swift red flesh, a winter king—
Who squired the glacier woman down the sky?
She ran the neighing canyons all the spring;
She spouted arms; she rose with maize—to die.

And in the autumn drouth, whose burnished hands
With mineral wariness found out the stone
Where prayers, forgotten, streamed the mesa sands?
He holds the twilight's dim, perpetual throne.

Mythical brows we saw retiring—loth,
Disturbed and destined, into denser green.
Greeting they sped us, on the arrow's oath:
Now lie incorrigibly what years between . . .

There was a bed of leaves, and broken play;
There was a veil upon you, Pocahontas, bride—
O Princess whose brown lap was virgin May;
And bridal flanks and eyes hid tawny pride.

I left the village for dogwood. By the canoe
Tugging below the mill-race, I could see
Your hair's keen crescent running, and the blue
First moth of evening take wing stealthily.

What laughing chains the water wove and threw!
I learned to catch the trout's moon whisper; I
Drifted how many hours I never knew,
But, watching, saw that fleet young crescent die,—

*Then you shall
see her truly
—your blood
remembering
its first
invasion of her
secrecy, its
first encounters
with her kin,
her chieftain
lover . . . his
shade that
haunts the
lakes and hills*

And one star, swinging, take its place, alone,
Cupped in the larches of the mountain pass—
Until, immortally, it bled into the dawn.
I left my sleek boat nibbling margin grass . . .

I took the portage climb, then chose
A further valley-shed; I could not stop.
Feet nozzled wat'ry webs of upper flows;
One white veil gusted from the very top.

O Appalachian Spring! I gained the ledge;
Steep, inaccessible smile that eastward bends
And northward reaches in that violet wedge
Of Adirondacks!—wisped of azure wands,

Over how many bluffs, tarns, streams I sped!
—And knew myself within some boding shade:—
Grey tepees tufting the blue knolls ahead,
Smoke swirling through the yellow chestnut glade . . .

A distant cloud, a thunder-bud—it grew,
That blanket of the skies: the padded foot
Within,—I heard it; 'til its rhythm drew,
—Siphoned the black pool from the heart's hot root!

A cyclone threshes in the turbine crest,
Swooping in eagle feathers down your back;
Know, Maquokeeta, greeting; know death's best;
—Fall, Sachem, strictly as the tamarack!

A birch kneels. All her whistling fingers fly.
The oak grove circles in a crash of leaves;
The long moan of a dance is in the sky.
Dance, Maquokeeta: Pocahontas grieves . . .

And every tendon scurries toward the twangs
Of lightning deltaed down your saber hair.
Now snaps the flint in every tooth; red fangs
And splay tongues thinly busy the blue air . . .

Dance, Maquokeeta! snake that lives before,
That casts his pelt, and lives beyond! Sprout, horn!
Spark, tooth! Medicine-man, relent, restore—
Lie to us,—dance us back the tribal morn!

Spears and assemblies: black drums thrusting on—
O yelling battlements,—I, too, was liege
To rainbows currying each pulsant bone:
Surpassed the circumstance, danced out the siege!

And buzzard-circleted, screamed from the stake;
I could not pick the arrows from my side.
Wrapped in that fire, I saw more escorts wake—
Flickering, sprint up the hill groins like a tide.

I heard the hush of lava wrestling your arms,
And stag teeth foam about the raven throat;
Flame cataracts of heaven in seething swarms
Fed down your anklets to the sunset's moat.

O, like the lizard in the furious noon,
That drops his legs and colors in the sun,
—And laughs, pure serpent, Time itself, and moon
Of his own fate, I saw thy change begun!

And saw thee dive to kiss that destiny
Like one white meteor, sacrosanct and blent
At last with all that's consummate and free
There, where the first and last gods keep thy tent.

*   *   *

Thewed of the levin, thunder-shod and lean,
Lo, through what infinite seasons dost thou gaze—
Across what bivouacs of thine angered slain,
And see'st thy bride immortal in the maize!

Totem and fire-gall, slumbering pyramid—
Though other calendars now stack the sky,
Thy freedom is her largesse, Prince, and hid
On paths thou knewest best to claim her by.

High unto Labrador the sun strikes free
Her speechless dream of snow, and stirred again,
She is the torrent and the singing tree;
And she is virgin to the last of men . . .

West, west and south! winds over Cumberland
And winds across the llano grass resume
Her hair's warm sibilance. Her breasts are fanned
O stream by slope and vineyard—into bloom!

And when the caribou slant down for salt
Do arrows thirst and leap? Do antlers shine
Alert, star-triggered in the listening vault
Of dusk?—And are her perfect brows to thine?

We danced, O Brave, we danced beyond their farms,
In cobalt desert closures made our vows . . .
Now is the strong prayer folded in thine arms,
The serpent with the eagle in the boughs.

INDIANA

The morning glory, climbing the morning long
  Over the lintel on its wiry vine,
Closes before the dusk, furls in its song
     As I close mine . . .

And bison thunder rends my dreams no more
  As once my womb was torn, my boy, when you
Yielded your first cry at the prairie's door . . .
     Your father knew

Then, though we'd buried him behind us, far
  Back on the gold trail—then his lost bones
    stirred . . .
But you who drop the scythe to grasp the oar
     Knew not, nor heard.

How we, too, Prodigal, once rode off, too—
  Waved Seminary Hill a gay good-bye . . .
We found God lavish there in Colorado
     But passing sly.

The pebbles sang, the firecat slunk away
  And glistening through the sluggard freshets came
In golden syllables loosed from the clay
     His gleaming name.

*. . . and read
her in a
mother's
farewell gaze.*

77

A dream called Eldorado was his town,
  It rose up shambling in the nuggets' wake,
It had no charter but a promised crown
      Of claims to stake.

But we,—too late, too early, howsoever—
  Won nothing out of fifty-nine—those years—
But gilded promise, yielded to us never,
      And barren tears . . .

The long trail back! I huddled in the shade
  Of wagon-tenting looked out once and saw
Bent westward, passing on a stumbling jade
      A homeless squaw—

Perhaps a halfbreed. On her slender back
  She cradled a babe's body, riding without rein.
Her eyes, strange for an Indian's, were not black
      But sharp with pain

And like twin stars. They seemed to shun the gaze
  Of all our silent men—the long team line—
Until she saw me—when their violet haze
      Lit with love shine . . .

I held you up—I suddenly the bolder,
  Knew that mere words could not have brought us
      nearer.
She nodded—and that smile across her shoulder
      Will still endear her

As long as Jim, your father's memory, is warm.
  Yes, Larry, now you're going to sea, remember
You were the first—before Ned and this farm,—
      First-born, remember—

And since then—all that's left to me of Jim
    Whose folks, like mine, came out of Arrowhead.
And you're the only one with eyes like him—
            Kentucky bred!

I'm standing still, I'm old, I'm half of stone!
    Oh, hold me in those eyes' engaging blue;
There's where the stubborn years gleam and atone,—
            Where gold is true!

Down the dim turnpike to the river's edge—
    Perhaps I'll hear the mare's hoofs to the ford . . .
Write me from Rio . . . and you'll keep your pledge;
            I know your word!

Come back to Indiana—not too late!
    (Or will you be a ranger to the end?)
Good-bye . . . Good-bye . . . oh, I shall always wait
    You, Larry, traveller—
                stranger,
                    son,
                        —my friend—

III

Cutty Sark

> *O, the navies old and oaken,*
> *O, the Temeraire no more!*
>
> **MELVILLE**

I met a man in South Street, tall—
a nervous shark tooth swung on his chain.
His eyes pressed through green grass
—green glasses, or bar lights made them
so—
    shine—
        GREEN—
            eyes—
stepped out—forgot to look at you
or left you several blocks away—

in the nickel-in-the-slot piano jogged
"Stamboul Nights"—weaving somebody's nickel—
       sang—

    O Stamboul Rose—dreams weave the rose!

        Murmurs of Leviathan he spoke,
        and rum was Plato in our heads . . .

"It's S.S. *Ala*—Antwerp—now remember kid
to put me out at three she sails on time.
I'm not much good at time any more keep
weakeyed watches sometimes snooze—" his bony hands
got to beating time . . . "A whaler once—
I ought to keep time and get over it—I'm a
Democrat—I know what time it is—No
I don't want to know what time it is—that
damned white Arctic killed my time . . ."

O Stamboul Rose—drums weave—

"I ran a donkey engine down there on the Canal
in Panama—got tired of that—
then Yucatan selling kitchenware—beads—
have you seen Popocatepetl—birdless mouth
with ashes sifting down—?
                         and then the coast again . . ."

Rose of Stamboul O coral Queen—
teased remnants of the skeletons of cities—
and galleries, galleries of watergutted lava
snarling stone—green—drums—drown—

Sing!
"—that spiracle!" he shot a finger out the door . . .
"O life's a geyser—beautiful—my lungs—
No—I can't live on land—!"

I saw the frontiers gleaming of his mind;
or are there frontiers—running sands sometimes
running sands—somewhere—sands running . . .
Or they may start some white machine that sings.
Then you may laugh and dance the axletree—
steel—silver—kick the traces—and know—

ATLANTIS ROSE drums wreathe the rose,
the star floats burning in a gulf of tears
and sleep another thousand—

                         interminably
long since somebody's nickel—stopped—
playing—

83

A wind worried those wicker-neat lapels, the
swinging summer entrances to cooler hells . . .
Outside a wharf truck nearly ran him down
—he lunged up Bowery way while the dawn
was putting the Statue of Liberty out—that
torch of hers you know—

I started walking home across the Bridge . . .

        *   *   *

Blithe Yankee vanities, turreted sprites, winged
                          British repartees, skil-
ful savage sea-girls
that bloomed in the spring—Heave, weave
those bright designs the trade winds drive . . .

> *Sweet opium and tea, Yo-ho!*
> *Pennies for porpoises that bank the keel!*
> *Fins whip the breeze around Japan!*

Bright skysails ticketing the Line, wink round the
    Horn
to Frisco, Melbourne . . .
                    Pennants, parabolas—
clipper dreams indelible and ranging,
baronial white on lucky blue!

    Perennial-*Cutty*-trophied-*Sark!*

Thermopylæ, *Black Prince*, *Flying Cloud* through
    Sunda
—scarfed of foam, their bellies veered green espla-
    nades,
locked in wind-humors, ran their eastings down;

at Java Head freshened the nip
(*sweet opium and tea!*)
and turned and left us on the lee . . .

Buntlines tusseling (91 days, 20 hours and anchored!)
Rainbow, Leander
(last trip a tragedy)—where can you be
Nimbus? and you rivals two—

a long tack keeping—

Taeping?
Ariel?

IV

Cape Hatteras

The seas all crossed,
weathered the capes, the voyage done . . .
WALT WHITMAN

Imponderable the dinosaur
            sinks slow,
                     the mammoth saurian
                              ghoul, the eastern
                                        Cape . . .
While rises in the west the coastwise range,
                     slowly the hushed land—
Combustion at the astral core—the dorsal change
Of energy—convulsive shift of sand . . .
But we, who round the capes, the promontories
Where strange tongues vary messages of surf
Below grey citadels, repeating to the stars
The ancient names—return home to our own
Hearths, there to eat an apple and recall
The songs that gypsies dealt us at Marseille
Or how the priests walked—slowly through Bombay—
Or to read you, Walt,—knowing us in thrall

To that deep wonderment, our native clay
Whose depth of red, eternal flesh of Pocahontas—
Those continental folded æons, surcharged
With sweetness below derricks, chimneys, tunnels—
Is veined by all that time has really pledged us . . .
And from above, thin squeaks of radio static,
The captured fume of space foams in our ears—
What whisperings of far watches on the main
Relapsing into silence, while time clears
Our lenses, lifts a focus, resurrects
A periscope to glimpse what joys or pain
Our eyes can share or answer—then deflects
Us, shunting to a labyrinth submersed
Where each sees only his dim past reversed . . .

But that star-glistered salver of infinity,
The circle, blind crucible of endless space,
Is sluiced by motion,—subjugated never.
Adam and Adam's answer in the forest
Left Hesperus mirrored in the lucid pool.
Now the eagle dominates our days, is jurist
Of the ambiguous cloud. We know the strident rule
Of wings imperious . . . Space, instantaneous,
Flickers a moment, consumes us in its smile:
A flash over the horizon—shifting gears—
And we have laughter, or more sudden tears.
Dream cancels dream in this new realm of fact
From which we wake into the dream of act;
Seeing himself an atom in a shroud—
Man hears himself an engine in a cloud!

"—Recorders ages hence"—ah, syllables of faith!
Walt, tell me, Walt Whitman, if infinity
Be still the same as when you walked the beach
Near Paumanok—your lone patrol—and heard the
    wraith
Through surf, its bird note there a long time
    falling . . .
For you, the panoramas and this breed of towers,
Of you—the theme that's statured in the cliff.
O Saunterer on free ways still ahead!
Not this our empire yet, but labyrinth
Wherein your eyes, like the Great Navigator's without
    ship,
Gleam from the great stones of each prison crypt
Of canyoned traffic . . . Confronting the Exchange,
Surviving in a world of stocks,—they also range
Across the hills where second timber strays
Back over Connecticut farms, abandoned pastures,—
Sea eyes and tidal, undenying, bright with myth!

The nasal whine of power whips a new universe . . .
Where spouting pillars spoor the evening sky,
Under the looming stacks of the gigantic power house
Stars prick the eyes with sharp ammoniac proverbs,
New verities, new inklings in the velvet hummed
Of dynamos, where hearing's leash is strummed . . .
Power's script,—wound, bobbin-bound, refined—
Is stropped to the slap of belts on booming spools,
　　　spurred
Into the bulging bouillon, harnessed jelly of the stars.
Towards what? The forked crash of split thunder parts
Our hearing momentwise; but fast in whirling arma-
　　　tures,
As bright as frogs' eyes, giggling in the girth
Of steely gizzards—axle-bound, confined
In coiled precision, bunched in mutual glee
The bearings glint,—O murmurless and shined
In oilrinsed circles of blind ecstasy!

Stars scribble on our eyes the frosty sagas,
The gleaming cantos of unvanquished space . . .
O sinewy silver biplane, nudging the wind's withers!
There, from Kill Devils Hill at Kitty Hawk
Two brothers in their twinship left the dune;
Warping the gale, the Wright windwrestlers veered
Capeward, then blading the wind's flank, banked and
　　　spun
What ciphers risen from prophetic script,
What marathons new-set between the stars!
The soul, by naphtha fledged into new reaches
Already knows the closer clasp of Mars,—
New latitudes, unknotting, soon give place
To what fierce schedules, rife of doom apace!

Behold the dragon's covey—amphibian, ubiquitous
To hedge the seaboard, wrap the headland, ride
The blue's cloud-templed districts unto ether . . .
While Iliads glimmer through eyes raised in pride
Hell's belt springs wider into heaven's plumed side.
O bright circumferences, heights employed to fly
War's fiery kennel masked in downy offings,—
This tournament of space, the threshed and chiselled
        height,
Is baited by marauding circles, bludgeon flail
Of rancorous grenades whose screaming petals carve us
Wounds that we wrap with theorems sharp as hail!

Wheeled swiftly, wings emerge from larval-silver
        hangars.
Taut motors surge, space-gnawing, into flight;
Through sparkling visibility, outspread, unsleeping,
Wings clip the last peripheries of light . . .
Tellurian wind-sleuths on dawn patrol,
Each plane a hurtling javelin of winged ordnance,
Bristle the heights above a screeching gale to hover;
Surely no eye that Sunward Escadrille can cover!
There, meaningful, fledged as the Pleiades
With razor sheen they zoom each rapid helix!
Up-chartered choristers of their own speeding
They, cavalcade on escapade, shear Cumulus—
Lay siege and hurdle Cirrus down the skies!
While Cetus-like, O thou Dirigible, enormous Lounger
Of pendulous auroral beaches,—satellited wide
By convoy planes, moonferrets that rejoin thee
On fleeing balconies as thou dost glide,
—Hast splintered space!

                        Low, shadowed of the Cape,
Regard the moving turrets! From grey decks
See scouting griffons rise through gaseous crepe
Hung low . . . until a conch of thunder answers
Cloud-belfries, banging, while searchlights, like
          fencers,
Slit the sky's pancreas of foaming anthracite
Toward thee, O Corsair of the typhoon,—pilot, hear!
Thine eyes bicarbonated white by speed, O Skygak, see
How from thy path above the levin's lance
Thou sowest doom thou hast nor time nor chance
To reckon—as thy stilly eyes partake
What alcohol of space . . . ! Remember, Falcon-Ace,
Thou hast there in thy wrist a Sanskrit charge
To conjugate infinity's dim marge—
Anew . . . !

                        But first, here at this height receive
The benediction of the shell's deep, sure reprieve!
Lead-perforated fuselage, escutcheoned wings
Lift agonized quittance, tilting from the invisible brink
Now eagle-bright, now

                              quarry-hid, twist-
                                        -ing, sink with
Enormous repercussive list-
                              -ings down
Giddily spiralled
                        gauntlets, upturned, unlooping
In guerrilla sleights, trapped in combustion gyr-
Ing, dance the curdled depth
                              down whizzing
Zodiacs, dashed
              (now nearing fast the Cape!)
                        down gravitation's
                              vortex into crashed

. . . . dispersion . . . into mashed and shapeless debris. . . .

By Hatteras bunched the beached heap of high bravery!

* * *

The stars have grooved our eyes with old persuasions
Of love and hatred, birth,—surcease of nations . . .
But who has held the heights more sure than thou,
O Walt!—Ascensions of thee hover in me now
As thou at junctions elegiac, there, of speed
With vast eternity, dost wield the rebound seed!
The competent loam, the probable grass,—travail
Of tides awash the pedestal of Everest, fail
Not less than thou in pure impulse inbred
To answer deepest soundings! O, upward from the
    dead
Thou bringest tally, and a pact, new bound
Of living brotherhood!

                    Thou, there beyond—
Glacial sierras and the flight of ravens,
Hermetically past condor zones, through zenith havens
Past where the albatross has offered up
His last wing-pulse, and downcast as a cup
That's drained, is shivered back to earth—thy wand
Has beat a song, O Walt,—there and beyond!
And this, thine other hand, upon my heart
Is plummet ushered of those tears that start
What memories of vigils, bloody, by that Cape,—
Ghoul-mound of man's perversity at balk
And fraternal massacre! Thou, pallid there as chalk,
Hast kept of wounds, O Mourner, all that sum
That then from Appomattox stretched to Somme!

Cowslip and shad-blow, flaked like tethered foam
Around bared teeth of stallions, bloomed that spring
When first I read thy lines, rife as the loam
Of prairies, yet like breakers cliffward leaping!
O, early following thee, I searched the hill
Blue-writ and odor-firm with violets, 'til
With June the mountain laurel broke through green
And filled the forest with what clustrous sheen!
Potomac lilies,—then the Pontiac rose,
And Klondike edelweiss of occult snows!
White banks of moonlight came descending valleys—
How speechful on oak-vizored palisades,
As vibrantly I following down Sequoia alleys
Heard thunder's eloquence through green arcades
Set trumpets breathing in each clump and grass tuft—
       'til
Gold autumn, captured, crowned the trembling hill!

Panis Angelicus! Eyes tranquil with the blaze
Of love's own diametric gaze, of love's amaze!
Not greatest, thou,—not first, nor last,—but near
And onward yielding past my utmost year.
Familiar, thou, as mendicants in public places;
Evasive—too—as dayspring's spreading arc to trace
       is:—
Our Meistersinger, thou set breath in steel;
And it was thou who on the boldest heel
Stood up and flung the span on even wing
Of that great Bridge, our Myth, whereof I sing!

Years of the Modern! Propulsions toward what capes?
But thou, *Panis Angelicus*, hast thou not seen
And passed that Barrier that none escapes—
But knows it leastwise as death-strife?—O, something
       green,
Beyond all sesames of science was thy choice

94

Wherewith to bind us throbbing with one voice,
New integers of Roman, Viking, Celt—
Thou, Vedic Caesar, to the greensward knelt!

And now, as launched in abysmal cupolas of space,
Toward endless terminals, Easters of speeding light—
Vast engines outward veering with seraphic grace
On clarion cylinders pass out of sight
To course that span of consciousness thou'st named
The Open Road—thy vision is reclaimed!
What heritage thou'st signalled to our hands!

And see! the rainbow's arch—how shimmeringly stands
Above the Cape's ghoul-mound, O joyous seer!
Recorders ages hence, yes, they shall hear
In their own veins uncancelled thy sure tread
And read thee by the aureole 'round thy head
Of pasture-shine, *Panis Angelicus!*

                                        yes, Walt,
Afoot again, and onward without halt,—
Not soon, nor suddenly,—no, never to let go
    My hand
                in yours,
                    Walt Whitman—

                                    so—

V

Three Songs

The one Sestos, the other Abydos hight.
MARLOWE

SOUTHERN CROSS

I wanted you, nameless Woman of the South,
No wraith, but utterly—as still more alone
The Southern Cross takes night
And lifts her girdles from her, one by one—
High, cool,
              wide from the slowly smoldering fire
Of lower heavens,—
                vaporous scars!

Eve! Magdalene!
          or Mary, you?

Whatever call—falls vainly on the wave.
O simian Venus, homeless Eve,
Unwedded, stumbling gardenless to grieve
Windswept guitars on lonely decks forever;
Finally to answer all within one grave!

And this long wake of phosphor,
                      iridescent
Furrow of all our travel—trailed derision!
Eyes crumble at its kiss. Its long-drawn spell
Incites a yell. Slid on that backward vision
The mind is churned to spittle, whispering hell.

I wanted you . . . The embers of the Cross
Climbed by aslant and huddling aromatically.
It is blood to remember; it is fire
To stammer back . . . It is
God—your namelessness. And the wash—

98

All night the water combed you with black
Insolence. You crept out simmering, accomplished.
Water rattled that stinging coil, your
Rehearsed hair—docile, alas, from many arms.
Yes, Eve—wraith of my unloved seed!

The Cross, a phantom, buckled—dropped below the
    dawn.
Light drowned the lithic trillions of your spawn.

NATIONAL WINTER GARDEN

Outspoken buttocks in pink beads
Invite the necessary cloudy clinch
Of bandy eyes. . . . No extra mufflings here:
The world's one flagrant, sweating cinch.

And while legs waken salads in the brain
You pick your blonde out neatly through the smoke.
Always you wait for someone else though, always—
(Then rush the nearest exit through the smoke).

Always and last, before the final ring
When all the fireworks blare, begins
A tom-tom scrimmage with a somewhere violin,
Some cheapest echo of them all—begins.

And shall we call her whiter than the snow?
Sprayed first with ruby, then with emerald sheen—
Least tearful and least glad (who knows her smile?)
A caught slide shows her sandstone grey between.

Her eyes exist in swivellings of her teats,
Pearls whip her hips, a drench of whirling strands.
Her silly snake rings begin to mount, surmount
Each other—turquoise fakes on tinselled hands.

We wait that writhing pool, her pearls collapsed,
—All but her belly buried in the floor;
And the lewd trounce of a final muted beat!
We flee her spasm through a fleshless door. . . .

Yet, to the empty trapeze of your flesh,
O Magdalene, each comes back to die alone.
Then you, the burlesque of our lust—and faith,
Lug us back lifeward—bone by infant bone.

VIRGINIA

O rain at seven,
Pay-check at eleven—
Keep smiling the boss away,
Mary (what are you going to do?)
Gone seven—gone eleven,
And I'm still waiting you—

O blue-eyed Mary with the claret scarf,
Saturday Mary, mine!

It's high carillon
From the popcorn bells!
Pigeons by the million—
And Spring in Prince Street
Where green figs gleam
By oyster shells!

O Mary, leaning from the high wheat tower,
Let down your golden hair!

High in the noon of May
On cornices of daffodils
The slender violets stray.
Crap-shooting gangs in Bleecker reign,
Peonies with pony manes—
Forget-me-nots at windowpanes:

Out of the way-up nickel-dime tower shine,
Cathedral Mary,
shine!—

VI

Quaker Hill

> *I see only the ideal. But no
> ideals have ever been fully suc-
> cessful on this earth.*
> **ISADORA DUNCAN**

> *The gentian weaves her fringes,
> The maple's loom is red.*
> **EMILY DICKINSON**

Perspective never withers from their eyes;
They keep that docile edict of the Spring
That blends March with August Antarctic skies:
These are but cows that see no other thing
Than grass and snow, and their own inner being
Through the rich halo that they do not trouble
Even to cast upon the seasons fleeting
Though they should thin and die on last year's stubble.

And they are awkward, ponderous and uncoy . . .
While we who press the cider mill, regarding them—
We, who with pledges taste the bright annoy
Of friendship's acid wine, retarding phlegm,
Shifting reprisals ('til who shall tell us when
The jest is too sharp to be kindly?) boast
Much of our store of faith in other men
Who would, ourselves, stalk down the merriest ghost.

Above them old Mizzentop, palatial white
Hostelry—floor by floor to cinquefoil dormer
Portholes the ceilings stack their stoic height.
Long tiers of windows staring out toward former
Faces—loose panes crown the hill and gleam
At sunset with a silent, cobwebbed patience . . .
See them, like eyes that still uphold some dream
Through mapled vistas, cancelled reservations!

High from the central cupola, they say
One's glance could cross the borders of three states;
But I have seen death's stare in slow survey
From four horizons that no one relates . . .

Weekenders avid of their turf-won scores,
Here three hours from the semaphores, the Czars
Of golf, by twos and threes in plaid plusfours
Alight with sticks abristle and cigars.

This was the Promised Land, and still it is
To the persuasive suburban land agent
In bootleg roadhouses where the gin fizz
Bubbles in time to Hollywood's new love-nest pageant.
Fresh from the radio in the old Meeting House
(Now the New Avalon Hotel) volcanoes roar
A welcome to highsteppers that no mouse
Who saw the Friends there ever heard before.

What cunning neighbors history has in fine!
The woodlouse mortgages the ancient deal
Table that Powitzky buys for only nine-
Ty five at Adams' auction,—eats the seal,
The spinster polish of antiquity . . .
Who holds the lease on time and on disgrace?
What eats the pattern with ubiquity?
Where are my kinsmen and the patriarch race?

The resigned factions of the dead preside.
Dead rangers bled their comfort on the snow;
But I must ask slain Iroquois to guide
Me farther than scalped Yankees knew to go:
Shoulder the curse of sundered parentage,
Wait for the postman driving from Birch Hill
With birthright by blackmail, the arrant page
That unfolds a new destiny to fill. . . .

So, must we from the hawk's far stemming view,
Must we descend as worm's eye to construe
Our love of all we touch, and take it to the Gate
As humbly as a guest who knows himself too late,

His news already told? Yes, while the heart is wrung,
Arise—yes, take this sheaf of dust upon your tongue!
In one last angelus lift throbbing throat—
Listen, transmuting silence with that stilly note

Of pain that Emily, that Isadora knew!
While high from dim elm-chancels hung with dew,
That triple-noted clause of moonlight—
Yes, whip-poor-will, unhusks the heart of fright,
Breaks us and saves, yes, breaks the heart, yet yields
That patience that is armour and that shields
Love from despair—when love foresees the end—
Leaf after autumnal leaf
                          break off,
                                    descend—
                                              descend—

VII

The Tunnel

To Find the Western path
Right thro' the Gates of Wrath.

BLAKE

Performances, assortments, résumés—
Up Times Square to Columbus Circle lights
Channel the congresses, nightly sessions,
Refractions of the thousand theatres, faces—
Mysterious kitchens. . . . You shall search them all.
Someday by heart you'll learn each famous sight
And watch the curtain lift in hell's despite;
You'll find the garden in the third act dead,
Finger your knees—and wish yourself in bed
With tabloid crime-sheets perched in easy sight.

    Then let you reach your hat
    and go.
    As usual, let you—also
    walking down—exclaim
    to twelve upward leaving
    a subscription praise
    for what time slays.

Or can't you quite make up your mind to ride;
A walk is better underneath the L a brisk
Ten blocks or so before? But you find yourself
Preparing penguin flexions of the arms,—
As usual you will meet the scuttle yawn:
The subway yawns the quickest promise home.

Be minimum, then, to swim the hiving swarms
Out of the Square, the Circle burning bright—
Avoid the glass doors gyring at your right,

Where boxed alone a second, eyes take fright
—Quite unprepared rush naked back to light:
And down beside the turnstile press the coin
Into the slot. The gongs already rattle.

> And so
> of cities you bespeak
> subways, rivered under streets
> and rivers. . . . In the car
> the overtone of motion
> underground, the monotone
> of motion is the sound
> of other faces, also underground—

"Let's have a pencil Jimmy—living now
at Floral Park
Flatbush—on the fourth of July—
like a pigeon's muddy dream—potatoes
to dig in the field—travlin the town—too—
night after night—the Culver line—the
girls all shaping up—it used to be—"

Our tongues recant like beaten weather vanes.
This answer lives like verdigris, like hair
Beyond extinction, surcease of the bone;
And repetition freezes—"What

"what do you want? getting weak on the links?
fandaddle daddy don't ask for change—IS THIS
FOURTEENTH? it's half past six she said—if
you don't like my gate why did you
swing on it, why *didja*
swing on it
anyhow—"

> And somehow anyhow swing—

The phonographs of hades in the brain
Are tunnels that re-wind themselves, and love
A burnt match skating in a urinal—
Somewhere above Fourteenth TAKE THE EXPRESS
To brush some new presentiment of pain—

"But I want service in this office SERVICE
I said—after
the show she cried a little afterwards but—"

Whose head is swinging from the swollen strap?
Whose body smokes along the bitten rails,
Bursts from a smoldering bundle far behind
In back forks of the chasms of the brain,—
Puffs from a riven stump far out behind
In interborough fissures of the mind . . . ?

And why do I often meet your visage here,
Your eyes like agate lanterns—on and on
Below the toothpaste and the dandruff ads?
—And did their riding eyes right through your side,
And did their eyes like unwashed platters ride?
And Death, aloft,—gigantically down
Probing through you—toward me, O evermore!
And when they dragged your retching flesh,
Your trembling hands that night through Baltimore—
That last night on the ballot rounds, did you
Shaking, did you deny the ticket, Poe?

For Gravesend Manor change at Chambers Street.
The platform hurries along to a dead stop.

The intent escalator lifts a serenade
Stilly
Of shoes, umbrellas, each eye attending its shoe, then
Bolting outright somewhere above where streets

Burst suddenly in rain. . . . The gongs recur:
Elbows and levers, guard and hissing door.
Thunder is galvothermic here below. . . . The car
Wheels off. The train rounds, bending to a scream,
Taking the final level for the dive
Under the river—
And somewhat emptier than before,
Demented, for a hitching second, humps; then
Lets go. . . . Toward corners of the floor
Newspapers wing, revolve and wing.
Blank windows gargle signals through the roar.

And does the Dæmon take you home, also,
Wop washerwoman, with the bandaged hair?
After the corridors are swept, the cuspidors—
The gaunt sky-barracks cleanly now, and bare,
O Genoese, do you bring mother eyes and hands
Back home to children and to golden hair?

Dæmon, demurring and eventful yawn!
Whose hideous laughter is a bellows mirth
—Or the muffled slaughter of a day in birth—
O cruelly to inoculate the brinking dawn
With antennæ toward worlds that glow and sink;—
To spoon us out more liquid than the dim
Locution of the eldest star, and pack
The conscience navelled in the plunging wind,
Umbilical to call—and straightway die!

O caught like pennies beneath soot and steam,
Kiss of our agony thou gatherest;
Condensed, thou takest all—shrill ganglia
Impassioned with some song we fail to keep.
And yet, like Lazarus, to feel the slope,
The sod and billow breaking,—lifting ground,

111

—A sound of waters bending astride the sky
Unceasing with some Word that will not die . . . !

*　　　*　　　*

A tugboat, wheezing wreaths of steam,
Lunged past, with one galvanic blare stove up the
    River.
I counted the echoes assembling, one after one,
Searching, thumbing the midnight on the piers.
Lights, coasting, left the oily tympanum of waters;
The blackness somewhere gouged glass on a sky.
And this thy harbor, O my City, I have driven under,
Tossed　from　the　coil　of　ticking　towers. . . .
    Tomorrow,
And to be. . . . Here by the River that is East—
Here at the waters' edge the hands drop memory;
Shadowless in that abyss they unaccounting lie.
How far away the star has pooled the sea—
Or shall the hands be drawn away, to die?

Kiss of our agony Thou gatherest,
            O Hand of Fire
                gatherest—

VIII

Atlantis

Music is then the knowledge of that which relates to love in harmony and system.

PLATO

Through the bound cable strands, the arching path
Upward, veering with light, the flight of strings,—
Taut miles of shuttling moonlight syncopate
The whispered rush, telepathy of wires.
Up the index of night, granite and steel—
Transparent meshes—fleckless the gleaming staves—
Sibylline voices flicker, waveringly stream
As though a god were issue of the strings. . . .

And through that cordage, threading with its call
One arc synoptic of all tides below—
Their labyrinthine mouths of history
Pouring reply as though all ships at sea
Complighted in one vibrant breath made cry,—
"Make thy love sure—to weave whose song we ply!"
—From black embankments, moveless soundings
     hailed,
So seven oceans answer from their dream.

And on, obliquely up bright carrier bars
New octaves trestle the twin monoliths
Beyond whose frosted capes the moon bequeaths
Two worlds of sleep (O arching strands of song!)—
Onward and up the crystal-flooded aisle
White tempest nets file upward, upward ring
With silver terraces the humming spars,
The loft of vision, palladium helm of stars.

Sheerly the eyes, like seagulls stung with rime—
Slit and propelled by glistening fins of light—
Pick biting way up towering looms that press
Sidelong with flight of blade on tendon blade
—Tomorrows into yesteryear—and link
What cipher-script of time no traveller reads
But who, through smoking pyres of love and death,
Searches the timeless laugh of mythic spears.

Like hails, farewells—up planet-sequined heights
Some trillion whispering hammers glimmer Tyre:
Serenely, sharply up the long anvil cry
Of inchling æons silence rivets Troy.
And you, aloft there—Jason! hesting Shout!
Still wrapping harness to the swarming air!
Silvery the rushing wake, surpassing call,
Beams yelling Æolus! splintered in the straits!

From gulfs unfolding, terrible of drums,
Tall Vision-of-the-Voyage, tensely spare—
Bridge, lifting night to cycloramic crest
Of deepest day—O Choir, translating time
Into what multitudinous Verb the suns
And synergy of waters ever fuse, recast
In myriad syllables,—Psalm of Cathay!
O Love, thy white, pervasive Paradigm . . . !

We left the haven hanging in the night—
Sheened harbor lanterns backward fled the keel.
Pacific here at time's end, bearing corn,—
Eyes stammer through the pangs of dust and steel.
And still the circular, indubitable frieze
Of heaven's meditation, yoking wave
To kneeling wave, one song devoutly binds—
The vernal strophe chimes from deathless strings!

115

O Thou steeled Cognizance whose leap commits
The agile precincts of the lark's return;
Within whose lariat sweep encinctured sing
In single chrysalis the many twain,—
Of stars Thou art the stitch and stallion glow
And like an organ, Thou, with sound of doom—
Sight, sound and flesh Thou leadest from time's realm
As love strikes clear direction for the helm.

Swift peal of secular light, intrinsic Myth
Whose fell unshadow is death's utter wound,—
O River-throated—iridescently upborne
Through the bright drench and fabric of our veins;
With white escarpments swinging into light,
Sustained in tears the cities are endowed
And justified conclamant with ripe fields
Revolving through their harvests in sweet torment.

Forever Deity's glittering Pledge, O Thou
Whose canticle fresh chemistry assigns
To wrapt inception and beatitude,—
Always through blinding cables, to our joy,
Of thy white seizure springs the prophecy:
Always through spiring cordage, pyramids
Of silver sequel, Deity's young name
Kinetic of white choiring wings . . . ascends.

Migrations that must needs void memory,
Inventions that cobblestone the heart,—
Unspeakable Thou Bridge to Thee, O Love.
Thy pardon for this history, whitest Flower,
O Answerer of all,—Anemone,—
Now while thy petals spend the suns about us, hold—
(O Thou whose radiance doth inherit me)
Atlantis,—hold thy floating singer late!

So to thine Everpresence, beyond time,
Like spears ensanguined of one tolling star
That bleeds infinity—the orphic strings,
Sidereal phalanxes, leap and converge:
—One Song, one Bridge of Fire! Is it Cathay,
Now pity steeps the grass and rainbows ring
The serpent with the eagle in the leaves . . . ?
Whispers antiphonal in azure swing.

THREE

Uncollected Poems

I

Early Poems

THE MOTH THAT GOD MADE BLIND

Among cocoa-nut palms of a far oasis,
Conceived in the light of Arabian moons,
There are butterflies born in mosaic date-vases,
That emerge black and vermeil from yellow cocoons.

Some say that for sweetness they cannot see far,—
That their land is too gorgeous to free their eyes wide
To horizons which knife-like would only mar
Their joy with a barren and steely tide—

That they only can see when their moon limits vision,
Their mother, the moon, marks a halo of light
On their own small oasis, ray-cut, an incision,
Where are set all the myriad jewelleries of night.

So they sleep in the shade of black palm-bark at noon,
Blind only in day, but remembering that soon
She will flush their hid wings in the evening to blaze
Countless rubies and tapers in the oasis' blue haze.

But over one moth's eyes were tissues at birth
Too multiplied even to center his gaze
On that circle of paradise cool in the night;—
Never came light through that honey-thick glaze.

And had not his pinions with signs mystical
And rings macrocosmic won envy as thrall,
They had scorned him, so humbly low, bound there
     and tied
At night like a grain of sand, futile and dried.

122

But once though, he learned of that span of his
    wings,—
The florescence, the power he felt bud at the time
When the others were blinded by all waking things;
And he ventured the desert,—his wings took the climb.

And lo, in that dawn he was pierroting over,—
Swinging in spirals round the fresh breasts of day.
The moat of the desert was melting from clover
To yellow,—to crystal,—a sea of white spray—

Til the sun, he still gyrating, shot out all white,—
Though a black god to him in a dizzying night;—
And without one cloud-car in that wide meshless blue
The sun saw a ruby brightening ever, that flew.

Seething and rounding in long streams of light
The heat led the moth up in octopus arms:
The honey-wax eyes could find no alarms,
But they burned thinly blind like an orange peeled
    white.

And the torrid hum of great wings was his song
When below him he saw what his whole race had
    shunned—
Great horizons and systems and shores all along
Which blue tides of cool moons were slow shaken and
    sunned.

A little time only, for sight burned as deep
As his blindness before had frozen in Hell,
And his wings atom-withered,—gone,—left but a
    leap:—
To the desert,—back,—down,—still lonely he fell.

I have hunted long years for a spark in the sand;—
My eyes have hugged beauty and winged life's brief
    spell.
These things I have:—a withered hand;—
Dim eyes;—a tongue that cannot tell.

[1960]

C 33

He has woven rose-vines
About the empty heart of night,
And vented his long mellowed wines
Of dreaming on the desert white
With searing sophistry.
And he tended with far truths he would form
The transient bosoms from the thorny tree.

O Maternal to enrich thy gold head
And wavering shoulders with a new light shed

From penitence must needs bring pain,
And with it song of minor, broken strain.
But you who hear the lamp whisper thru night
Can trace paths tear-wet, and forget all blight.

[1916]

OCTOBER-NOVEMBER

Indian-summer-sun
With crimson feathers whips away the mists;
Dives through the filter of trellises
And gilds the silver on the blotched arbor-seats.

Now gold and purple scintillate
On trees that seem dancing
In delirium;
Then the moon
In a mad orange flare
Floods the grape-hung night.

[1916]

THE HIVE

Up the chasm-walls of my bleeding heart
Humanity pecks, claws, sobs and climbs;
Up the inside, and over every part
Of the hive of the world that is my heart.

And of all the sowing, and all the tear-tendering,
And reaping, have mercy and love issued forth.
Mercy, white milk, and honey, gold love—
And I watch, and say, "These the anguish are worth."

[1917]

FEAR

The host, he says that all is well,
And the fire-wood glow is bright;
The food has a warm and tempting smell,—
But on the window licks the night.

Pile on the logs. . . . Give me your hands,
Friends! No,—it is not fright. . . .
But hold me . . . somewhere I heard demands. . . .
And on the window licks the night.

[1917]

ANNUNCIATIONS

The anxious milk-blood in the veins of the earth,
That strives long and quiet to sever the girth
Of greenery. . . . Below the roots, a quickening shiver
Aroused by some light that had sensed,—ere the shiver
Of the first moth's descent,—day's predestiny. . . .
The sound of a dove's flight waved over the lawn. . . .
The moans of travail of one dearest beside me. . . .
Then high cries from great chasms of chaos out-
    drawn. . . .
Hush! these things were all heard before dawn.

[1917]

ECHOES

I

Slivers of rain upon the pane,
Jade-green with sunlight, melt and flow
Upward again:—they leave no stain
Of storm or strain an hour ago.

II

Over the hill a last cloud dips,
And disappears, as I should go
Silently, now, but that your lips
Are warmer with a redder glow.

III

Fresh and fragile, your arms now
Are circles of cool roses,—so. . . .
In opal pools beneath your brow
I dream we quarreled long, long ago.

[1917]

THE BATHERS

Two ivory women by a milky sea;—
The dawn, a shell's pale lining restlessly
Shimmering over a black mountain-spear:—
A dreamer might see these, and wake to hear,
But there is no sound,—not even a bird-note;
Only simple ripples flaunt, and stroke, and float,—
Flat lily petals to the sea's white throat.

They say that Venus shot through foam to light,
But they are wrong. . . . Ere man was given sight
She came in such still water, and so nursed
In silence, beauty blessed and beauty cursed.

[1917]

MODERN CRAFT

Though I have touched her flesh of moons,
Still she sits gestureless and mute,
Drowning cool pearls in alcohol.
O blameless shyness;—innocence dissolute!

She hazards jet; wears tiger-lilies;—
And bolts herself within a jewelled belt.
Too many palms have grazed her shoulders:
Surely she must have felt.

Ophelia had such eyes; but she
Even, sank in love and choked with flowers.
This burns and is not burnt. . . . My modern love
    were
Charred at a stake in younger times than ours.

[1918]

132

CARMEN DE BOHEME

Sinuously winding through the room
On smokey tongues of sweetened cigarettes,—
Plaintive yet proud the cello tones resume
The andante of smooth hopes and lost regrets.

Bright peacocks drink from flame-pots by the wall,
Just as absinthe-sipping women shiver through
With shimmering blue from the bowl in Circe's hall.
Their brown eyes blacken, and the blue drop hue.

The andante quivers with crescendo's start,
And dies on fire's birth in each man's heart.
The tapestry betrays a finger through
The slit, soft-pulling:— — — and music follows cue.

There is a sweep,—a shattering,—a choir
Disquieting of barbarous fantasy.
The pulse is in the ears, the heart is higher,
And stretches up through mortal eyes to see.

Carmen! Akimbo arms and smouldering eyes;—
Carmen! Bestirring hope and lipping eyes;—
Carmen whirls, and music swirls and dips.
"Carmen!," comes awed from wine-hot lips.

Finale leaves in silence to replume
Bent wings, and Carmen with her flaunts through the
    gloom
Of whispering tapestry, brown with old fringe:—
The winers leave too, and the small lamps twinge.

Morning: and through the foggy city gate
A gypsy wagon wiggles, striving straight.
And some dream still of Carmen's mystic face,—
Yellow, pallid, like ancient lace.

[1918]

CARRIER LETTER

My hands have not touched water since your hands,—
No;—nor my lips freed laughter since "farewell."
And with the day, distance again expands
Between us, voiceless as an uncoiled shell.

Yet,—much follows, much endures . . . Trust birds
    alone:
A dove's wings clung about my heart last night
With surging gentleness; and the blue stone
Set in the tryst-ring has but worn more bright.

[1918]

POSTSCRIPT

Though now but marble are the marble urns,
Though fountains droop in waning light and pain
Glitters on the edges of wet ferns,
I should not dare to let you in again.

Mine is a world foregone though not yet ended,—
An imagined garden grey with sundered boughs
And broken branches, wistful and unmended,
And mist that is more constant than your vows.

[1918]

FORGETFULNESS

Forgetfulness is like a song
That, freed from beat and measure, wanders.
Forgetfulness is like a bird whose wings are reconciled,
Outspread and motionless,—
A bird that coasts the wind unwearyingly.

Forgetfulness is rain at night,
Or an old house in a forest,—or a child.
Forgetfulness is white,—white as a blasted tree,
And it may stun the sybil into prophecy,
Or bury the Gods.

I can remember much forgetfulness.

[1918]

TO PORTAPOVITCH

(*du Ballet Russe*)

Vault on the opal carpet of the sun,
Barbaric Prince Igor:—or, blind Pierrot,
Despair until the moon by tears be won:—
Or, Daphnis, move among the bees with Chloe.

Release,—dismiss the passion from your arms.
More real than life, the gestures you have spun
Haunt the blank stage with lingering alarms,
Though silent as your sandals, danced undone.

[1919]

LEGENDE

The tossing loneliness of many nights
Rounds off my memory of her.
Like a shell surrendered to evening sands,
Yet called adrift again at every dawn,
She has become a pathos,—
Waif of the tides.

The sand and sea have had their way,
And moons of spring and autumn,—
All, save I.
And even my vision will be erased
As a cameo the waves claim again.

[1919]

INTERIOR

It sheds a shy solemnity,
This lamp in our poor room.
O grey and gold amenity,—
Silence and gentle gloom!

Wide from the world, a stolen hour
We claim, and none may know
How love blooms like a tardy flower
Here in the day's after-glow.

And even should the world break in
With jealous threat and guile,
The world, at last, must bow and win
Our pity and a smile.

[1919]

EPISODE OF HANDS

The unexpected interest made him flush.
Suddenly he seemed to forget the pain,—
Consented,—and held out
One finger from the others.

The gash was bleeding, and a shaft of sun
That glittered in and out among the wheels,
Fell lightly, warmly, down into the wound.

And as the fingers of the factory owner's son,
That knew a grip for books and tennis
As well as one for iron and leather,—
As his taut, spare fingers wound the gauze
Around the thick bed of the wound,
His own hands seemed to him
Like wings of butterflies
Flickering in sunlight over summer fields.

The knots and notches,—many in the wide
Deep hand that lay in his,—seemed beautiful.
They were like the marks of wild ponies' play,—
Bunches of new green breaking a hard turf.

And factory sounds and factory thoughts
Were banished from him by that larger, quieter hand
That lay in his with the sun upon it.
And as the bandage knot was tightened
The two men smiled into each other's eyes.

[1948]

THE BRIDGE OF ESTADOR

An Impromptu,

Aesthetic

TIRADE

Walk high on the bridge of Estador,
No one has ever walked there before.
There is a lake, perhaps, with the sun
Lapped under it,—or the dun
Bellies and estuaries of warehouses,
Tied bundle-wise with cords of smoke.

Do not think too deeply, and you'll find
A soul, an element in it all.

How can you tell where beauty's to be found?
I have heard hands praised for what they made;
I have heard hands praised for line on line;
Yet a gash with sunlight jerking through
A mesh of belts down into it, made me think
I had never seen a hand before.
And the hand was thick and heavily warted.

High on the bridge of Estador
Where no one has ever been before,—
I do not know what you'll see,—your vision
May slumber yet in the moon, awaiting
Far consummations of the tides to throw
Clean on the shore some wreck of dreams. . . .

But some are twisted with the love
Of things irreconcilable,—
The slant moon with the slanting hill:
O Beauty's fool, though you have never
Seen them again, you won't forget.
Nor the Gods that danced before you
When your fingers spread among stars.

And you others—follow your arches
To what corners of the sky they pull you to,—
The everlasting eyes of Pierrot,
  Or, of Gargantua, the laughter.

[1948]

143

PORPHYRO IN AKRON

I

Greeting the dawn,
A shift of rubber workers presses down
South Main.
With the stubbornness of muddy water
It dwindles at each cross-line
Until you feel the weight of many cars
North-bound, and East and West,
Absorbing and conveying weariness,—
Rumbling over the hills.

Akron, "high place",—
A bunch of smoke-ridden hills
Among rolling Ohio hills.

The dark-skinned Greeks grin at each other
In the streets and alleys.
The Greek grins and fights with the Swede,—
And the Fjords and the Aegean are remembered.

The plough, the sword,
The trowel,—and the monkey wrench!
O City, your axles need not the oil of song.
I will whisper words to myself
And put them in my pockets.
I will go and pitch quoits with old men
In the dust of a road.

And some of them "will be Americans,"
Using the latest ice-box and buying Fords;
And others—

I remember one Sunday noon,
Harry and I, "the gentlemen",—seated around
A table of raisin-jack and wine, our host
Setting down a glass and saying,—

"One month,—I go back rich.
I ride black horse. . . . Have many sheep."
And his wife, like a mountain, coming in
With four tiny black-eyed girls around her
Twinkling like little Christmas trees.

And some Sunday fiddlers,
Roumanian business men,
Played ragtime and dances before the door,
And we overpayed them because we felt like it.

Pull down the hotel counterpane
And hitch yourself up to your book.

"Full on this casement shone the wintry moon,
And threw warm gules on Madeline's fair breast,
As down she knelt for heaven's grace and boon . . ."

"Connais tu le pays . . . ?"

Your mother sang that in a stuffy parlour
One summer day in a little town
Where you had started to grow.
And you were outside as soon as you
Could get away from the company
To find the only rose on the bush
In the front yard. . . . . . .

But look up, Porphyro,—your toes
Are ridiculously tapping
The spindles at the foot of the bed.

The stars are drowned in a slow rain,
And a hash of noises is slung up from the street.
You ought, really, to try to sleep,
Even though, in this town, poetry's a
Bedroom occupation.

[1921]

146

A PERSUASION

If she waits late at night
Hearing the wind,
It is to gather kindnesses
No world can offer.

She has drawn her hands away.
The wind plays andantes
Of lost hopes and regrets,—
And yet is kind.

Below the wind,
Waiting for morning
The hills lie curved and blent
As now her heart and mind.

[1921]

LOCUTIONS DES PIERROTS

Translated from the French of Jules Laforgue

I

Your eyes, those pools with soft rushes,
O prodigal and wholly dilatory lady,
Come now, when will they restore me
The orient moon of my dapper affections?

For imminent is that moment when,
Because of your perverse austerities,
My crisp soul will be flooded by a languor
Bland as the wide gaze of a Newfoundland.

Ah, madame! truly it's not right
When one isn't the real Gioconda,
To adaptate her methods and deportment
For snaring the poor world in a blue funk.

II

Ah! the divine infatuation
That I nurse for Cydalise
Now that she has fled the capture
Of my lunar sensibility!

True, I nibble at despondencies
Among the flowers of her domain
To the sole end of discovering
What is her unique propensity!

—Which is to be mine, you say?
Alas, you know how much I oppose
A stiff denial to postures
That seem too much impromptu.

III

Ah! without the moon, what white nights,
What nightmares rich with ingenuity!
Don't I see your white swans there?
Doesn't someone come to turn the knob?

And it's your fault that I'm this way.
That my conscience sees double,
And my heart fishes in troubled water
For Eve, Gioconda and Dalila.

Oh, by the infinite circumflex
Of the archbeam of my cross-legged labours,
Come now—appease me just a little
With the why-and-wherefore of Your Sex!

[1922]

THE GREAT WESTERN PLAINS

The little voices of prairie dogs
Are tireless . . .
They will give three hurrahs
Alike to stage, equestrian, and pullman,
And all unstintingly as to the moon.

And Fifi's bows and poodle ease
Whirl by them centred in the lap
Of Lottie Honeydew, movie queen,
Toward lawyers and Nevada.

And how much more they cannot see!
Alas, there is so little time,
The world moves by so fast these days!
Burrowing in silk is not their way—
And yet they know the tomahawk.

Indeed, old memories come back to life;
Pathetic yelps have sometimes greeted
Noses pressed against the glass.

[1922]

AMERICA'S PLUTONIC ECSTASIES

(With homage to E. E. Cummings)

preferring laxatives to wine
all america is saying
"how are my bowels today?" and
feeling them in every way and
peering
for the one goat (unsqueezable)
that kicked out long ago—

or, even thinking
of something—Oh!
unbelievably—Oh!
HEADY!—those aromatic LEMONS!
that make your colored syrup fairly
PULSE!—yes, PULSE!

the nation's lips are thin and fast
with righteousness and yet if
memory serves there is still
catharsis from gin-daisies as well as
maidenhairferns, and the BRONX
doesn't stink at all.

       These
and other natural grammarians are ab-
so-loot-lee necessary
for a FREEEE-er PASSAGE—(NOT
to india, o ye faithful,
but a little BACK DOOR DIGNITY)

[1923]

INTERLUDIUM

To "La Montagne" by Lachaise

Thy time is thee to wend
with languor such as gains
immensity in gathered grace; the arms
to spread; the hands to yield their shells

and fostering
thyself, bestow to thee
illimitable and unresigned
(no instinct flattering vainly now)

Thyself
that heavens climb to measure, thus
unfurling thee untried,—until
from sleep forbidden now and wide
partitions in thee—goes

communicant and speeding new
the cup again wide from thy throat to spend
those streams and slopes untenanted thou
hast known. . . . And blithe

Madonna, natal to thy yielding
still subsist I, wondrous as
from thine open dugs shall still the sun
again round one more fairest day.

[1924]

152

II

Late Poems

Key West:

An Island Sheaf

The starry floor,
The wat'ry shore,
Is given thee 'til the break of day.
BLAKE

O CARIB ISLE!

The tarantula rattling at the lily's foot
Across the feet of the dead, laid in white sand
Near the coral beach—nor zigzag fiddle crabs
Side-stilting from the path (that shift, subvert
And anagrammatize your name)—No, nothing here
Below the palsy that one eucalyptus lifts
In wrinkled shadows—mourns.

               And yet suppose
I count these nacreous frames of tropic death,
Brutal necklaces of shells around each grave
Squared off so carefully. Then

To the white sand I may speak a name, fertile
Albeit in a stranger tongue. Tree names, flower names
Deliberate, gainsay death's brittle crypt. Meanwhile
The wind that knots itself in one great death—
Coils and withdraws. So syllables want breath.

But where is the Captain of this doubloon isle
Without a turnstile? Who but catchword crabs
Patrols the dry groins of the underbrush?
What man, or What
Is Commissioner of mildew throughout the ambushed
    senses?
His Carib mathematics web the eyes' baked lenses!

Under the poinciana, of a noon or afternoon
Let fiery blossoms clot the light, render my ghost
Sieved upward, white and black along the air
Until it meets the blue's comedian host.

Let not the pilgrim see himself again
For slow evisceration bound like those huge terrapin
Each daybreak on the wharf, their brine-caked eyes;
—Spiked, overturned; such thunder in their strain!
And clenched beaks coughing for the surge again!

Slagged of the hurricane—I, cast within its flow,
Congeal by afternoons here, satin and vacant.
You have given me the shell, Satan,—carbonic amulet
Sere of the sun exploded in the sea.

[1927]

THE MERMEN

> *And if*
> *Thy banished trunk be found in our dominions—*
> KING LEAR

Buddhas and engines serve us undersea;
Though why they bide here, only hell that's sacked
Of every blight and ingenuity—
Can solve.

      The Cross alone has flown the wave.
But since the Cross sank, much that's warped and
    cracked
Has followed in its name, has heaped its grave.
Oh—

Gallows and guillotines to hail the sun
And smoking racks for penance when day's done!
No—

Leave us, you idols of Futurity—alone,
Here where we finger moidores of spent grace
And ponder the bright stains that starred this Throne

—This Cross, agleam still with a human Face!

[1928]

TO THE CLOUD JUGGLER

In Memoriam: Harry Crosby

What you may cluster 'round the knees of space
We hold in vision only, asking trace
Of districts where cliff, sea and palm advance
The falling wonder of a rainbow's trance.

Your light lifts whiteness into virgin azure . . .
Disclose your lips, O Sun, nor long demure
With snore of thunder, crowding us to bleed
The green preëmption of the deep seaweed.

You, the rum-giver to that slide-by-night,—
The moon's best lover,—guide us by a sleight
Of quarts to faithfuls—surely smuggled home—
As you raise temples fresh from basking foam.

Expose vaunted validities that yawn
Past pleasantries . . . Assert the ripened dawn
As you have yielded balcony and room
Or tempests—in a silver, floating plume.

Wrap us and lift us; drop us then, returned
Like water, undestroyed,—like mist, unburned . . .
But do not claim a friend like him again,
Whose arrow must have pierced you beyond pain.

[1930]

THE MANGO TREE

Let them return, saying you blush again for the great
Great-grandmother. It's all like Christmas.

When you sprouted Paradise a discard of chewing-
gum took place. Up jug to musical, hanging jug just gay
spiders yoked you first,—silking of shadows good under-
drawers for owls.

First-plucked before and since the Flood, old hypno-
tisms wrench the golden boughs. Leaves spatter dawn
from emerald cloud-sprockets. Fat final prophets with
lean bandits crouch: and dusk is close
                    under your noon,
                    you Sun-heap, whose
ripe apple-lanterns gush history, recondite lightnings,
irised.

                    O mister Señor
                    missus Miss
                    Mademoiselle
                    with baskets

                                        Maggy, come on

                                        [1929]

160

ISLAND QUARRY

Square sheets—they saw the marble only into
Flat prison slabs there at the marble quarry
At the turning of the road around the roots of the
    mountain
Where the straight road would seem to ply below the
    stone, that fierce
Profile of marble spiked with yonder
Palms against the sunset's towering sea, and maybe
Against mankind. It is at times—

In dusk, as though this island lifted, floated
In Indian baths. At Cuban dusk the eyes
Walking the straight road toward thunder—
This dry road silvering toward the shadow of the
    quarry
—It is at times as though the eyes burned hard and
    glad
And did not take the goat path quivering to the right,
Wide of the mountain—thence to tears and sleep—
But went on into marble that does not weep.

[1927]

OLD SONG

Thy absence overflows the rose,—
    From every petal gleam
Such words as it were vain to close,
    Such tears as crowd the dream.

So eyes that mind thee fair and gone,
    Bemused at waking, spend
On skies that gild thy remote dawn
    More hopes than here attend.

The burden of the rose will fade
    Sped in the spectrum's kiss.
But here the thorn in sharpened shade
    Weathers all loneliness.

[1927]

THE IDIOT

Sheer over to the other side,—for see—
The boy straggling under those mimosas, daft
With squint lanterns in his head, and it's likely
Fumbling his sex. That's why those children laughed

In such infernal circles round his door
Once when he shouted, stretched in ghastly shape.
I hurried by. But back from the hot shore
Passed him again . . . He was alone, agape;

One hand dealt out a kite string, a tin can
The other tilted, peeled end clapped to eye.
That kite aloft—you should have watched him scan
Its course, though he'd clamped midnight to noon sky!

And since, through these hot barricades of green,
A *Dios gracias, graç*—I've heard his song
Above all reason lifting, halt serene—
My trespass vision shrinks to face his wrong.

[1927]

163

A NAME FOR ALL

Moonmoth and grasshopper that flee our page
And still wing on, untarnished of the name
We pinion to your bodies to assuage
Our envy of your freedom—we must maim

Because we are usurpers, and chagrined—
And take the wing and scar it in the hand.
Names we have, even, to clap on the wind;
But we must die, as you, to understand.

I dreamed that all men dropped their names, and sang
As only they can praise, who build their days
With fin and hoof, with wing and sweetened fang
Struck free and holy in one Name always.

[1929]

164

BACARDI SPREADS THE
EAGLE'S WINGS

"Pablo and Pedro, and black Serafin
Bought a launch last week. It might as well
Have been made of—well, say paraffin,—
That thin and blistered . . . just a rotten shell.

"Hell! out there among the barracudas
Their engine stalled. No oars, and leaks
Oozing a-plenty. They sat like baking Buddhas.
Luckily the Cayman schooner streaks

"By just in time, and lifts 'em high and dry . . .
They're back now on that mulching job at Pepper's.
—Yes, patent-leather shoes hot enough to fry
Anyone but these native high-steppers!"

[1927]

IMPERATOR VICTUS

Big guns again
No speakee well
But plain.

Again, again—
And they shall tell
The Spanish Main

The Dollar from the Cross.

Big guns again.
But peace to thee,
Andean brain.

Again, again—
Peace from his Mystery
The King of Spain,

That defunct boss.

Big guns again,
Atahualpa,
Imperator Inca—

Slain.

[1933]

ROYAL PALM

For Grace Hart Crane

Green rustlings, more-than-regal charities
Drift coolly from that tower of whispered light.
Amid the noontide's blazed asperities
I watched the sun's most gracious anchorite

Climb up as by communings, year on year
Uneaten of the earth or aught earth holds,
And the grey trunk, that's elephantine, rear
Its frondings sighing in ætherial folds.

Forever fruitless, and beyond that yield
Of sweat the jungle presses with hot love
And tendril till our deathward breath is sealed—
It grazes the horizons, launched above

Mortality—ascending emerald-bright,
A fountain at salute, a crown in view—
Unshackled, casual of its azured height
As though it soared suchwise through heaven too.

[1927]

THE AIR PLANT

Grand Cayman

This tuft that thrives on saline nothingness,
Inverted octopus with heavenward arms
Thrust parching from a palm-bole hard by the cove—
A bird almost—of almost bird alarms,

Is pulmonary to the wind that jars
Its tentacles, horrific in their lurch.
The lizard's throat, held bloated for a fly,
Balloons but warily from this throbbing perch.

The needles and hack-saws of cactus bleed
A milk of earth when stricken off the stalk;
But this,—defenseless, thornless, sheds no blood,
Almost no shadow—but the air's thin talk.

Angelic Dynamo! Ventriloquist of the Blue!
While beachward creeps the shark-swept Spanish
       Main
By what conjunctions do the winds appoint
Its apotheosis, at last—the hurricane!

[1928]

THE HURRICANE

Lo, Lord, Thou ridest!
Lord, Lord, Thy swifting heart

Nought stayeth, nought now bideth
But's smithereened apart!

Ay! Scripture flee'th stone!
Milk-bright, Thy chisel wind

Rescindeth flesh from bone
To quivering whittlings thinned—

Swept, whistling straw! Battered,
Lord, e'en boulders now outleap

Rock sockets, levin-lathered!
Nor, Lord, may worm outdeep

Thy drum's gambade, its plunge abscond!
Lord God, while summits crashing

Whip sca-kclp screaming on blond
Sky-seethe, dense heaven dashing—

Thou ridest to the door, Lord!
Thou bidest wall nor floor, Lord!

[1927, 1931]

TO EMILY DICKINSON

You who desired so much—in vain to ask—
Yet fed your hunger like an endless task,
Dared dignify the labor, bless the quest—
Achieved that stillness ultimately best,

Being, of all, least sought for: Emily, hear!
O sweet, dead Silencer, most suddenly clear
When singing that Eternity possessed
And plundered momently in every breast;

—Truly no flower yet withers in your hand,
The harvest you descried and understand
Needs more than wit to gather, love to bind.
Some reconcilement of remotest mind—

Leaves Ormus rubyless, and Ophir chill.
Else tears heap all within one clay-cold hill.

[1927]

KEY WEST

Here has my salient faith annealed me.
Out of the valley, past the ample crib
To skies impartial, that do not disown me
Nor claim me, either, by Adam's spine—nor rib.

The oar plash, and the meteorite's white arch
Concur with wrist and bicep. In the moon
That now has sunk I strike a single march
To heaven or hades—to an equally frugal noon.

Because these millions reap a dead conclusion
Need I presume the same fruit of my bone
As draws them towards a doubly mocked confusion
Of apish nightmares into steel-strung stone?

O, steel and stone! But gold was, scarcity before.
And here is water, and a little wind. . . .
There is no breath of friends and no more shore
Where gold has not been sold and conscience tinned.

[1933]

171

—AND BEES OF PARADISE

I had come all the way here from the sea,
Yet met the wave again between your arms
Where cliff and citadel—all verily
Dissolved within a sky of beacon forms—

Sea gardens lifted rainbow-wise through eyes
I found.

      Yes, tall, inseparably our days
Pass sunward. We have walked the kindled skies
Inexorable and girded with your praise,

By the dove filled, and bees of Paradise.

[1933]

172

MOMENT FUGUE

The syphilitic selling violets calmly
    and daisies
By the subway news-stand knows
        how hyacinths

This April morning offers
    hurriedly
In bunches sorted freshly—
       and bestows
On every purchaser
         (of heaven perhaps)

His eyes—
      like crutches hurtled against glass
Fall mute and sudden (dealing change
    for lilies)
Beyond the roses that no flesh can pass.

[1929]

173

BY NILUS ONCE I KNEW . . .

Some old Egyptian joke is in the air,
Dear lady—the poet said—release your hair;
Come, search the marshes for a friendly bed
Or let us bump heads in some lowly shed.

An old Egyptian jest has cramped the tape.
The keyboard no more offers an escape
From the sweet jeopardy of Anthony's plight:
You've overruled my typewriter tonight.

Decisive grammar given unto queens,—
An able text, more motion than machines
Have levers for,—stampede it with fresh type
From twenty alphabets—we're still unripe!

This hieroglyph is no dumb, deaf mistake.
It knows its way through India—tropic shake!
It's Titicaca till we've trod it through
And then it pleads again, "I wish I knew."

[1933]

III

More Late Poems

THE VISIBLE THE UNTRUE

To E. O.

Yes, I being
the terrible puppet of my dreams, shall
lavish this on you—
the dense mine of the orchid, split in two[,]
And the fingernails that cinch such
environs?
And what about the staunch neighbor tabulations,
with all their zest for doom?

I'm wearing badges
that cancel all your kindness. Forthright
I watch the silver Zeppelin
destroy the sky. To
stir your confidence?
To rouse what sanctions—?

The silver strophe . . . the canto
bright with myth . . . Such
distances leap landward without
evil smile. And, as for me. . . .

The window weight throbs in its blind
partition. To extinguish what I have of faith.
Yes, light. And it is always
always, always the eternal rainbow
And it is always the day, the farewell day unkind.

[1933]

176

REPLY

Thou canst read nothing except through appetite
And here we join eyes in that sanctity
Where brother passes brother without sight,
But finally knows conviviality . . .

Go then, unto thy turning and thy blame.
Seek bliss then, brother, in my moment's shame.
All this that balks delivery through words
Shall come to you through wounds prescribed by
    swords:

That hate is but the vengeance of a long caress,
And fame is pivotal to shame with every sun
'That rises on eternity's long willingness . . .
So sleep, dear brother, in my fame, my shame undone.

[1933]

THE PHANTOM BARK

So dream thy sails, O phantom bark
That I thy drownèd man may speak again
Perhaps as once Will Collins spoke the lark,
And leave me half adream upon the main.

For who shall lift head up to funnel smoke,
And who trick back the leisured winds again
As they were fought—and wooed? They now but stoke
Their vanity, and dream no land in vain.

Of old there was a promise, and thy sails
Have kept no faith but wind, the cold stream
—The hot fickle wind, the breath of males
Imprisoned never, no[,] not soot &[?] steam[. . . .]

[1933]

LENSES

In the focus of the evening there is this island with
the buzz of saw mills, the crunch and blast of quarries;
furnaces, chisels and ploughs.

And the idiot boy by the road, with carbonated eyes, laughing or extending a phallus through the grating,—talking to
a kite high in the afternoon, or in the twilight scanning
pebbles among cinders in the road through a twice-opened
tomato can.

And there is work, blood, suet and sweat,—the rigamarole
of wine and mandolines. Midnight; and maybe love . . .

And there is, as Mr. Budge explained before his
chorea took him away—there is the Nine of
three-times-three, the hopeful plasm,
the vigilance of the ape, the repetition of the parrot. Locks on
doors and lips of agony to
dance upon. And there is

time for these; time for all these, as cattle and birds
know, Mr.
Budge—
why did
you
die
so
soon
?

There is
this gate of
wrath

[1948]

179

TO LIBERTY

Out of the seagull cries and wind
On this strange shore I build
The virgin. They laugh to hear
How I endow her, standing
Hair mocked by the sea, her lover
A dead sailor that knew
Not even Helen's fame.

Light the last torch in the wall,
The sea wall. Bring her no robes yet.
They have not seen her in this harbor;
Eyes widely planted, clear, yet small.
And must they overcome the fog,
Or must we rend our dream?

[1948]

ETERNITY

September — remember!
October—all over.
BARBADIAN ADAGE

After it was over, though still gusting balefully,
The old woman and I foraged some drier clothes
And left the house, or what was left of it;
Parts of the roof reached Yucatan, I suppose.
She almost—even then—got blown across lots
At the base of the mountain. But the town, the town!

Wires in the streets and Chinamen up and down
With arms in slings, plaster strewn dense with tiles,
And Cuban doctors, troopers, trucks, loose hens . . .
The only building not sagging on its knees,
Fernandez' Hotel, was requisitioned into pens
For cotted negroes, bandaged to be taken
To Havana on the first boat through. They groaned.

But was there a boat? By the wharf's old site you saw
Two decks unsandwiched, split sixty feet apart
And a funnel high and dry up near the park
Where a frantic peacock rummaged amid heaped cans.
No one seemed to be able to get a spark
From the world outside, but some rumor blew
That Havana, not to mention poor Batabanó,
Was halfway under water with fires
For some hours since—all wireless down
Of course, there too.

                    Back at the erstwhile house
We shoveled and sweated; watched the ogre sun
Blister the mountain, stripped now, bare of palm,
Everything—and lick the grass, as black as patent
Leather, which the rimed white wind had glazed.
Everything gone—or strewn in riddled grace—
Long tropic roots high in the air, like lace.
And somebody's mule steamed, swaying right by the
        pump,
Good God! as though his sinking carcass there
Were death predestined! You held your nose already
along the roads, begging for buzzards, vultures . . .
The mule stumbled, staggered. I somehow couldn't
        budge
To lift a stick for pity of his stupor.

                                        For I
Remember still that strange gratuity of horses
—One ours, and one, a stranger, creeping up with
        dawn
Out of the bamboo brake through howling, sheeted
        light
When the storm was dying. And Sarah saw them,
        too—
Sobbed. Yes, now—it's almost over. For they know;
The weather's in their noses. There's Don—but that
        one, white
—I can't account for him! And true, he stood
Like a vast phantom maned by all that memoried
        night
Of screaming rain—Eternity!

                            Yet water, water!
I beat the dazed mule toward the road. He got that far
And fell dead or dying, but it didn't so much matter.

                    182

The morrow's dawn was dense with carrion hazes
Sliding everywhere. Bodies were rushed into graves
Without ceremony, while hammers pattered in town.
The roads were being cleared, injured brought in
And treated, it seemed. In due time
The President sent down a battleship that baked
Something like two thousand loaves on the way.
Doctors shot ahead from the deck in planes.
The fever was checked. I stood a long time in Mack's
    talking
New York with the gobs, Guantanamo, Norfolk,—
Drinking Bacardi and talking U.S.A.

                                         [1933]

TO THE EMPRESS JOSEPHINE'S STATUE

Martinique

Image of Constancy

You, who contain augmented tears, explosions[,]
Have kissed, caressed the model of the hurricane[,]
Gathered and made musical in feathery fronds
The slit eclipse of moon in palm-lit bonds[,]
Deny me not in this sweet Caribbean dawn[—]
You, who have looked back to Leda, who have seen the
    Swan[.]

I own it still—that sure deliberation—
Leave, leave that Caribbean praise to me
Who claims a devout concentration
To wage you surely back to memory[—]
Your generosity dispose relinquishment and care[.]
Thy death is sacred to all those who share
Love and the breath of faith, momentous bride[.]
You did not die for conquerors at your side
Nor that fruit of mating which is widowed pride[.]

[1948]

A POSTSCRIPT

Friendship agony! words came to me
at last shyly. My only final friends—
the wren and thrush, made solid print for me
across dawn's broken arc. No; yes . . . or were they
the audible ransom, ensign of my faith
toward something far, now farther than ever away?

Remember the lavender lilies of that dawn,
their ribbon miles, beside the railroad ties
as one nears New Orleans, sweet trenches by the train
after the western desert and the later cattle country;
and other gratuities, like porters[,] jokes, roses . . .

Dawn's broken arc! the noon's more furbished room!
Yet seldom was there faith in the heart's right kind-
        ness.
There were tickets and alarm clocks. There were
        counters and schedules;
and a paralytic woman on an island of the Indies,
Antillean fingers counting my pulse, my love forever.

[1933]

TO SHAKESPEARE

Through torrid entrances, past icy poles
   A hand moves on the page! Who shall again
Engrave such hazards as thy might controls—
   Conflicting, purposeful yet outcry vain
Of all our days, being pilot,—tempest, too!
   Sheets that mock lust and thorns that scribble hate
Are lifted from torn flesh with human rue,
   And laughter, burnished brighter than our fate[,]
Thou wieldest with such tears that every faction
   Swears high in Hamlet's throat, and devils throng
Where angels beg for doom in ghast distraction
   —And fail, both! Yet thine Ariel holds his song:
And that serenity that Prospero gains
Is justice that has cancelled earthly chains.

[1933]

MARCH

Awake to the cold light
of wet wind running
twigs in tremors. Walls
are naked. Twilights raw—
and when the sun taps steeples
their glistenings dwindle
upward . . .

March
slips along the ground
like a mouse under pussy
willows, a little hungry.

The vagrant ghost of winter,
is it this that keeps the chimney
busy still? For something still
nudges shingles and windows:

but waveringly,—this ghost,
this slate-eyed saintly wraith
of winter wanes
and knows its waning.

[1927]

187

HAVANA ROSE

Let us strip the desk for action—now we have a horse in Mexico. . . . That night in Vera Cruz—verily for me "the True Cross"—let us remember the Doctor and my thoughts, my humble, fond remembrances of the great bacteriologist. . . . The wind that night, the clamour of incessant shutters, trundle doors, and the cherub watchman—tiptoeing the successive patio balconies with a typical pistol—trying to muffle doors—and the pharos shine—the mid-wind midnight stroke of it, its milk-light regularity above my bath partition through the lofty, dusty glass—*Cortez—Cortez*—his crumbled palace in the square—the typhus in a trap, the Doctor's rat trap. Where? Somewhere in Vera Cruz—to bring—to take—to mix—to ransom—to deduct—*to cure.* . . . The rats played ring around the rosy (in their basement basinette)—the Doctor *supposedly* slept, supposedly in #35—thus in my wakeful watches at least—the lighthouse flashed . . . whirled . . . delayed, and struck—*again, again.* Only the Mayans surely slept—whose references to typhus and whose records spurred the Doctor into something nigh those metaphysics that are typhoid plus and had engaged him once before to death's beyond and back again—antagonistic wills—into immunity. Tact, horsemanship, courage were germicides to him. . . . Poets may not be doctors, but doctors are rare poets when roses leap like rats—and too, when rats make rose nozzles of pink death around white teeth. . . .

And during the wait over dinner at La Diana the

Doctor had said—who was American, also—"You cannot heed the negative—so might go on to undeserved doom . . . must therefore loose yourself within a pattern's mastery that you can conceive, that you can yield to—by which also you win and gain mastery and happiness which is your own from birth.["]

[1933]

RELIQUARY

Tenderness and resolution[!]
What is our life without a sudden pillow—
What is death without a ditch?

The harvest laugh of bright Apollo
And the flint tooth of Sagittarius
Rhyme from the same Tau (closing cinch by cinch)
And pocket us who, somehow, do not follow,
As though we knew (those who are variants[)]
Charms that each by each refuse the clinch

With desperate propriety, whose name is writ
In wider letters than the alphabet,—
Who is now left to vary the Sanscrit
Pillowed by

My wrist in the vestibule of time—who
Will hold it—wear the keepsake, dear, of time—
Return the mirage on a coin that spells
Something of sand and sun the Nile defends . . . [?]

[1933]

PURGATORIO

My country, O my land, my friends—
Am I apart—here from you in a land
Where all your gas lights—faces—sputum gleam
Like something left, forsaken—here am I—
And are these stars—the high plateau—the scents
Of Eden—and the dangerous tree—are these
The landscape of confession—and if confession
So absolution? Wake pines—but pines wake here.
I dream the too-keen cider—the too-soft snow.
Where are the bayonets that the scorpion may not
    grow[?]
Here quakes of earth make houses fall—
And all my countrymen I see rush toward one stall[.]
Exile is thus a purgatory—not such as Dante built

But rather like a blanket than a quilt—
And I have no decision—is it green or brown
That I prefer to country or to town[?]
I am unraveled, umbilical anew[,]
So ring the church bells here in Mexico—
(They ring too obdurately here to need my call)
And what hours they forget to chime I'll know
As one whose altitude at one time was not [. . .]

[1933]

THE SAD INDIAN

Sad heart, the gymnast of inertia, does not count
Hours, days—and scarcely sun and moon—
The warp is in the woof—and his keen vision
Spells what his tongue has had—and only that—
How more?—but the lash, lost vantage—and the prison
His fathers took for granted ages since—and so he
    looms

Farther than his sun-shadow—farther than wings
—Their shadows even—now can't carry him.
He does not know the new hum in the sky
And—backwards—is it thus the eagles fly?

[1933]

192

THE BROKEN TOWER

The bell-rope that gathers God at dawn
Dispatches me as though I dropped down the knell
Of a spent day—to wander the cathedral lawn
From pit to crucifix, feet chill on steps from hell.

Have you not heard, have you not seen that corps
Of shadows in the tower, whose shoulders sway
Antiphonal carillons launched before
The stars are caught and hived in the sun's ray?

The bells, I say, the bells break down their tower;
And swing I know not where. Their tongues engrave
Membrane through marrow, my long-scattered score
Of broken intervals . . . And I, their sexton slave!

Oval encyclicals in canyons heaping
The impasse high with choir. Banked voices slain!
Pagodas, campaniles with reveilles outleaping—
O terraced echoes prostrate on the plain! . . .

And so it was I entered the broken world
To trace the visionary company of love, its voice
An instant in the wind (I know not whither hurled)
But not for long to hold each desperate choice.

My word I poured. But was it cognate, scored
Of that tribunal monarch of the air
Whose thigh embronzes earth, strikes crystal Word
In wounds pledged once to hope—cleft to despair?

The steep encroachments of my blood left me
No answer (could blood hold such a lofty tower
As flings the question true?)—or is it she
Whose sweet mortality stirs latent power?—

And through whose pulse I hear, counting the strokes
My veins recall and add, revived and sure
The angelus of wars my chest evokes:
What I hold healed, original now, and pure . . .

And builds, within, a tower that is not stone
(Not stone can jacket heaven)—but slip
Of pebbles,—visible wings of silence sown
In azure circles, widening as they dip

The matrix of the heart, lift down the eye
That shrines the quiet lake and swells a tower . . .
The commodious, tall decorum of that sky
Unseals her earth, and lifts love in its shower.

[1932]

FOUR

Selected Prose

THE CASE AGAINST NIETZSCHE

Before the war, Nietzsche's writings were moderately popular in France, where he was hailed by the Sorbonne long before Oxford awoke to his dimensions. But now the French call him the herald of modern Prussianism.

How paradoxical their accusation seems, when we know that Nietzsche was drawn to the French temperament more than to any other. His favorite novelists were French; Pascal and Montaigne were sources which he frequently mentions as potent influences in his development. Goethe and Schopenhauer were the only Germans for whom he had philosophic ears; and these, as he declares, were fundamentally un-German.

And yet again, how can he be called the spokesman of a nation which always affected him with disgust,—if not with hatred? His epithets on characteristic "Germania" at times approach the unprintable. He even denied his German origin, and declared himself a Pole in all his views and sympathies. Anyone who can picture him as an inspired leader of legions of "the pigheaded,' as he called them, has indeed capacities for self-delusion.

I might refer to Par. 320 in *Menschliches, Allzumenschliches* for a direct arraignment of Prussianism, although no names are mentioned in it. Here the autocratic machine is coolly exposed. He cites the direct control by the state over all educational institutions; the inaccessibility to all personal distinction except through some service, sooner or later, to the state; compulsory military training; the supremacy of the army; and at the end he ironically observes,—"Then nothing more is wanted but an opportunity for great wars.

These are provided from professional reasons (and so in all innocence) by diplomats, aided by newspapers and Stock Exchanges. For the 'nation,' as a nation of soldiers, need never be supplied with a good conscience in war,—it has one already."

Nietzsche, Zeppelins, and poisoned-gas go ill together. But Great Indra! one may envy Nietzsche a little; think of being so elusive,—so mercurial, as to be first swallowed whole, then coughed up, and still remain a mystery!

[1918]

JOYCE AND ETHICS

The Los Angeles critic who commented on Joyce in the last issue was adequately answered, I realize,—but the temptation to emphasize such illiteracy, indiscrimination, and poverty still pulls a little too strongly for resistance.

I noticed that Wilde, Baudelaire, and Swinburne are "stacked up" beside Joyce as rivals in "decadence" and "intellect." I am not yet aware that Swinburne ever possessed much beyond his "art ears," although these were long enough, and adequate to all his beautiful, though often meaningless mouthings. His instability in criticism and every form of literature that did not depend almost exclusively on sound for effect and his irrelevant metaphors are notorious. And as to Wilde,— after his bundle of paradoxes has been sorted and conned,—very little evidence of intellect remains. "Decadence" is something much talked about, and sufficiently misconstrued to arouse interest in the works of any fool. Any change in form, viewpoint, or mannerism can be so abused by the offending party. Sterility is the only "decadence" I recognize. An abortion in art takes the same place as it does in society,—it deserves no recognition whatever,—it is simply outside. A piece of work is art, or it isn't: there is no neutral judgment.

However,—let Baudelaire and Joyce stand together, as much as any such thing in literary comparison will allow. The principal eccentricity evinced by both is a penetration into life common to only the greatest. If people resent a thrust which discovers some of their entrails to themselves, I can see no reason for resorting to indiscriminate comparisons, naming colours of the rainbow, or advertising the fact that they have recently been forced to recognize a few of their personal qualities. Those who are capable of being only mildly "shocked" very naturally term the cost a penny, but were they capable of paying a few pounds for the same thinking, experience and realization by and in themselves, they could reserve their pennies for work minor to Joyce's.

The most nauseating complaint against his work is that of immorality and obscenity. The character of Stephen Dedalus is all too good for this world. It takes a little experience,—a few reactions on his part to understand it, and could this have been accomplished in a detached hermitage, high above the mud, he would no doubt have preferred that residence. A *Portrait of the Artist as a Young Man*, aside from Dante, is spiritually the most inspiring book I have ever read. It is Bunyan raised to art, and then raised to the ninth power.

[1918]

REVIEW OF *THE GHETTO AND OTHER POEMS*

Extremities in the modern world clash in a close proximity, so that there is a finer, harder line than usual to divide them. There is a cruelty in this,—a kind of desperation that is dramatic. Science, grown uncontrollable, has assumed a grin that has more than threatened the supposed civilization that fed it; science has brought light,—but it threatens to destroy the idea of reverence, the source of all light. Its despotism recognizes no limits. In one sense it has become a gargoyle.

Lola Ridge's volume is eloquent with a dramatic "awareness," or a kind of sharp recognition, of these dominating aspects of her time.

Her poems are always vivid:

"Life thunders on. . . .

Over the black bridge
The line of lighted cars
Creeps like a monstrous serpent
Spooring gold. . . .

Watchman, what of the track?

Night. . . . silence. . . . stars. . . .
All's well!"

She is seldom immersed in herself,—she never seems to lose consciousness of surroundings. Quite naturally this treatment gives a dramatic quality to even such a personal utterance as,—"Submerged"—

"I have known only my own shallows—
Safe, plumber places,
Where I was wont to preen myself.

But for the abyss
I wanted a plank beneath
And horizons. . . .

I was afraid of the silence
And the slipping toe-hold. . . ."

The essential to all real poetry is in Miss Ridge's
work,—sincerity. Sometimes the "macabre intensity"
of her words suggest[s] a slight theatricality. Sometimes
a figure or construction is so amazingly brilliant, that
one suspicions it has been used for itself alone, and
that Miss Ridge has been tempted toward a barren
cleverness. That she has decided capacities for it is certain. I hope only, that if her course swerves still further that way, she will utilize the novel, or some such
form, other than poetry.

"The Ghetto" is representative of the best of Miss
Ridge's endowments. In some aspects it is like a minia-
ture "Comédie humaine," with the dominant note of
sadness that runs through Balzac's narratives so insistently.

I have spoken more of the social significance of Miss
Ridge's work than strictly aesthetic canons would probably admit, because I have felt the interpretive aspects
of her work to be its most brilliant facet. When work
is so widely and minutely reflective of its time, then,
certainly, other than questions of pure *aesthétique*
must be considered.

[1919]

REVIEW OF MINNA AND MYSELF

I think that many of these poems will endure though they will probably not be widely popular for the principal reason that they are too distinguished,— too peculiar. They will be classed as "minor poetry," which designation, by the way, is beginning to assume a far from depreciative connotation in these days of attempted epics in "the grand style" like Miss Amy Lowell's very journalistic *Can Grande's Castle*.

Bodenheim cultivates a more limited field. His poems are often little heaps of images in which the verbal element is subordinated, making for an essentially static and decorative quality. There are, however, a few that make me think of the swaying plume of tiny bubbles that an effervescent pill, dissolving in a glass of water, will make. For example:—

"Grey, drooping-shouldered bushes scrape the edges
Of bending swirls of yellow-white flowers.
So do my thoughts meet the wind-scattered color of
    you." etc.

But the static element generally predominates, as here:—

"An old silver church in a forest
Is my love for you.
The trees around it
Are words that I have stolen from your heart.
An old silver bell, the last smile you gave
Hangs at the top of my church.
It rings only when you come through the forest
And stand beside it . . ." etc.

Bodenheim believes that "pure poetry is the vibrant expression of everything clearly delicate and unattached with surface sentiment in the emotions of men toward themselves and nature . . . True poetry is the entering of delicately imaginative plateaus, unconnected with human beliefs or fundamental human feelings." I quote from his article in *The New Republic* of December 22nd, 1917. Now this definition seems to me inordinately precious. Fortunately for all he has not "lived up" to it, except in rare instances. A reaction to the general abuse of his art as a vehicle for all kinds of propaganda is responsible for this extremity of statement, I am sure.

In regard to the plays . . . I should prefer to call them tapestries, scenic rather than dramatic, in interest. Bodenheim is not a dramatist in the real sense of the term, and I question his possibilities in this field. But if he is to insist on incorporating such fine lines as are included in the conversation in *The Master Poisoner*, I think I should easily be won to listening. The most dramatic piece in the book, to my thinking, is the one called *Soldiers*, and that is so by virtue of arrangement,—a painful focus of realities.

[1919]

REVIEW OF *WINESBURG, OHIO*

Beyond an expression of intense gratitude to the author, it is hard to say a word in regard to a book such as Sherwood Anderson's *Winesburg, Ohio*. The entire paraphernalia of criticism is insignificant, erected against the walls of such a living monument as this book, so that defense and explanation are soon evident as its only office.

First of all, the book is Sherwood Anderson; then humanity, then a certain period in the development of America's "Middle West," so called, and finally, art. It is a great heart, in company with a strong hand, that can elicit the sympathy, or at least, the understanding of his auditor toward each and every one of the characters of his book; and it is in the nature of Sherwood Anderson, as it often was in Balzac, to accomplish it.

The spark that Edgar Lee Masters struck with his *Spoon River Anthology* was a mighty seedling of dynamite, cold and intense, but I might say sporadic, in comparison with the dignity, the "power in repose," and the sustained inner illumination and bloom of this book. There is the same infinite pathos here, but it seems curbed to a finer reticence that is more genuine than many of the portraits by the elder poet, which at times almost touch the melodramatic. However, there is no need to diminish the proportions of the adventurous discoverer in order to sufficiently praise the richness of the settler, for this, to me, seems the relationship in outlook, time, and performance, of these two Americans.

The Puritan that stalks through the swamps of "Spoon River" is manifest also in "Winesburg," but he is here a little less gaunt; I will not say more or less historically "true," although I do maintain that Sherwood Anderson, while typifying him strongly in local garments and habits, has nevertheless somewhat modified him with a certain beauty and suggestiveness of his universal recurrence in many ages. He is alive in a tale called "Godliness," but the beauty and innocence of youth escape him in terror. He plays parts in other episodes, but is by no means a preoccupation of the author. The windows, alleys, and lanes of the village are open to us to find what epics, tragedies, and idylls we may. There is everlasting beauty in a scene called "Mother." The ironic humor and richness of "An Awakening" are unmatched in anything I know of. "Queer" is a story that carries De Maupassant into an anti-climax of grating cogs; and "Paper Pills," perhaps the finest and most exquisite thing in the book, is so utterly new, that I know nothing with which to compare it, except, perhaps, an idyll of Lucretius.

To end with aesthetic considerations, the style is flawless. I know of no finer selection of "significant material," combined with proper treatment and economy of detail. America should read this book on her knees. It constitutes an important chapter in the Bible of her consciousness.

[1919]

A NOTE ON MINNS

An ignorance of the professional, technical "elements" of photography, it seems to me, should very slightly, if at all, invalidate one's claim to the appreciation of such work as that of H. W. Minns. In his case, my appreciation can begin only where the fundamental pedagogics of the camera leave off,—at the point where the craftsman merges into the artist,—where the creative element becomes distinct. Some combination of eye and sympathy and hand are subtly responsible for the quality in his work. His "arrangements" are not the empty, obvious contortions of so many modern photographers. He plainly could not content himself with that. There is, in his faces, the urge of an ethical curiosity and sympathy as strongly evident as in the novels of Henry James. Undoubtedly his portraits are deeper, more vivid, than the daily repetitions of his sitters in their mirrors give back to any but themselves, but this is only to mention again the creative element that gives to his portraits such a sense of dramatic revelations.

Mr. Minns has often exhibited in Europe, and has received extensive recognition at Dresden, Vienna, and Copenhagen exhibitions. He began taking pictures when he was considerably beyond thirty, and has since spent some twenty years working in the rather limited and unresponsive locality of Akron, Ohio.

[1920]

SHERWOOD ANDERSON

We have come a long way from the pattern-making preoccupations of a Henry James when we can welcome a statement from an artist with as bold a contrasting simplicity as the answer that Sherwood Anderson once gave me to an analysis I had attempted of one of his short stories. "I am in truth mighty little interested in any discussions of art or life, or what a man's place in the scheme of things may be. It has to be done, I suppose, but after all there is the *fact* of life. Its story wants telling and singing. That's what I want, —the tale and the song of it." And it is that Anderson has so pre-eminently captured the "tale and the song of it" that I find his words so acceptable—at least in so far as they relate to his own work.

I spoke of an "attempted" analysis because of being since satisfied that beyond the possibility of a certain uneven surface penetration, Anderson's stories possess a too defiant and timeless solidity,—too much a share of life and clay itself,—to be tagged and listed with mechanical precisions. And what a satisfaction this is, to read stories over and again without a bundle of dry bones and cogwheels of "situations" and "plots" spilling out into one's lap. It must have been because of a surfeit of such disappointments that *Winesburg, Ohio*, when it first appeared, kept me up a whole night in a steady crescendo of emotions. Here was "stark realism," but a realism simplified and strangely sophisticated by the inscrutable soil. And by "soil" I mean something much more than a kind of local colour. There is plenty of that quite wonderfully applied, both in *Winesburg* and in *Poor White*, but there is also something more important and rare than this,—a contact with animal and earthy life so indefinably yet powerfully used as a very foundation to the stories that it might be compared to the sap that pervades the tree-trunk, branches, and twigs. Let me quote an instance of what I mean from *Poor White*.

Clara Butterworth, merging into womanhood, is musing in the shadows of her father's barn. . . .

Clara jumped quickly out of the hammock and walked about under the trees in the orchard. Her thoughts of Jim Priest's youth startled her. It was as though she had walked suddenly into a room where a man and woman were making love. Her cheeks burned and her hands trembled. As she walked slowly through the clumps of grass and weeds that grew between the trees where the sunlight struggled through, bees coming home to the hives heavily laden with honey flew in droves about her head. There was something heady and purposeful about the song of labor that arose out of the beehives. It got into her blood and her step quickened. The words of Jim Priest that kept running through her head seemed a part of the same song the bees were singing. "The sap has begun to run up the tree," she repeated aloud. How significant and strange the words seemed! They were the kind of words a lover might use in speaking to his beloved. She had read many novels, but they contained no such words. It was better so. It was better to hear them from human lips.

This is but one of many remembered paragraphs and pages from which arises a lyricism, deliberate and light, as a curl of milkweed seeds drawn toward the sun. It is his love for rows of corn on flat lands, fields bending over rolling Ohio hills, and the smell of barns under the warm hours of noon, that has given Anderson's descriptions of modern city life, with its mechanical distortions of humanity, such thrust and bite.

In *Poor White* there is the "machine" of modern existence,—the monster that is upon us all. No one who treats however slightly of the lives of the poor or middle classes can escape the issues of its present hold on us. It has seduced the strongest from the land to the cities, and in most cases made empty and meaningless their lives. It has cheapened the worth of all human commodities and even the value of human lives. It has destroyed the pride and pleasure of the craftsman in his work. "Hugh McVey," the son of a tramp of sordid Missouri River life, becomes a "dreamer of the machines" who invents one after another typical practical improvement[s] such as harvesters, potato-planters, etc., which enrich the speculating manufacturers who grasp at them, bow down before them, and wrangle about them. McVey goes on inventing and himself making money, but finds himself in time becoming more and more indifferent and disappointed. Most of all he is bewildered by the ever greater rush of the new industrialism with its "becoming" towns, its smoke and squalor. He has found no satisfactory foothold. His own machines have robbed him of something and left nothing in its place. He cannot be satisfied with himself as a machine producing machines. Unconsciously he is being urged by more natural impulses that he has perhaps denied too long. Like so many others he is lost among cogs and complicated springs. One sees all through this book how character is bent, blunted, regulated, diverted, or lacerated by the "machine." There is the perfect episode of a harness-maker whose love for manual perfection of craft finally drives him to the murder of an upstart apprentice who had insisted in over-ruling him by adopting machine-made saddles as substitutes for the carefully wrought saddles of the old man.

Looking back at two earlier books, *Windy McPherson's Son* and *Marching Men*, one can see a great advance in *Poor White*. There has always been the propagandist threatening the artist in Anderson; and in these first two books the propagandist comes out too dangerously near a victory to satisfy us despite the much brilliant description these books contain. Since then he has freed himself from much of this. Not that he has chosen to ignore any fact[s] or problems, but rather that he has succeeded in treating them more impersonally, incorporating them, less obviously, in character and action. To appreciate this advance from the seductive stagnations of sentimentality to a clear acceptance and description of our life to-day for what it be worth, is to realize how few other Americans have had the courage, let alone the vision, to do anything like it. Norris and Dreiser, and one or two others of native birth, have been the only ones. In Anderson there has been some great sincerity, perhaps the element of the "soil" itself personified in him, that has made him refuse to turn aside to offer the crowds those profitable "lollypops" that have "made" and ruined so many other of our writers.

Of course it is patent that people do not like to be told the truth. Especially our Puritans! *Winesburg* was the first book to tell the truth about our small midwestern towns. And what a fury it threw some people into! It seemed to be so much easier for those people to fling back,—"Neuroticism!" "Obscenity!" and "Exaggeration!" than to recognize themselves and others there. I could understand it perfectly myself, having lived for a while in a small town of similar location and colour. But my real point for admiring it was not because it merely told the truth; it was that *Winesburg* represented a work of distinct aesthetic achievement, an example of synthetic form,—not merely a medley of a thousand exterior details such as Lewis's *Main Street*. It takes more than the recognition of facts as facts to move us in fiction. There must be some beauty wrung from them to hold us long. We can recognize this quality without having it pointed out to us if our hearts are not too deadened, our sensibilities too dulled. In *Winesburg*, the windows, alleys, and lanes of the place are opened to us to find what we may. There is an exalting pathos in the episode called "Mother." The ironic humor and richness of "An Awakening" has the vivid and unbroken vitality of a silhouette. "Paper Pills," to me the finest thing in the book, has an idyllic beauty that sets it beside the old legend of "Daphnis and Chloe," and there are other chapters and episodes unmatched anywhere.

During the last two years there have been some short stories published in various magazines, such as "I Want to Know Why," "The Triumph of the Egg," "The New Englander," and "The Other Woman," that I look forward to seeing collected into a volume. I would like to see Anderson handle the negro in fiction. So far it has not been done by anyone without sentimentality or cruelty, but the directness of his vision would produce something new and deep in this direction. In the winter and spring of '20 Anderson was in southern Alabama near the sea finishing *Poor White*, and his interest in the black man became so aroused that he wrote me,—"The negroes are the living wonder of this place. What a tale if someone could penetrate into the home and the life of the Southern negro and not taint it in the ordinary superficial way."

The time has already arrived when Anderson is beginning to be recognized as among the few first recorders of the life of a people coming to some state of self-consciousness. He is without sentimentality; and he makes no pretense of offering solutions. He has a humanity and simplicity that is quite baffling in depth and suggestiveness, and his steady and deliberate growth is proving right along the promise it gives of finer work. A verse from his "A New Testament" has an oddly personal tone to it:

My mind is the mind of a little man with thin legs who sells cigars in a store. My mind is the mind of a cripple who died in an alleyway at Cleveland, Ohio. My mind is the mind of a child who fell into a well, the mind of one who cleans the streets of a city, of an actor who walks up and down on a stage.

[1921]

REVIEW OF *EIGHT MORE HARVARD POETS*

The main bulk of this collection credits Harvard with little more than an even gait with recent Oxford and Cambridge anthologies of similar intention, and helps to prove that there are as many incipient "Georgians" in America as in England. The fact would hardly warrant mention if beyond this margin of quietude there were not the more animated gestures of two poets who have at least convincing manners. The attenuated Woodberrian echoes still haunt the banks of the Charles, but beside the fresher reactions of Malcolm Cowley and John Brooks Wheelwright even the disguise of vers libre fails to rescue their notes from the embrace of familiar nostalgias and worn allusions.

In this well-bred and predominating group (whose tradition certainly needs no present defense), Royall Snow is the only one to approach an interesting idiom. He has a rather true sense for classic diction, though he fails to carry his expression through to the point of valor. Like the others, he gives scattered couplets that are pleasant and all-too-quotable, but there is scarcely a poem from any of the six poets of this group which is satisfying as a completed statement.

A genial pedestrianism, however, in several of Malcolm Cowley's poems indicates the possibility of a 20th century "pastoral" form. A faculty for fresh record, city and road panorama, and ironic nuance, all make Cowley's experiments quite valuable. For one who can so well afford to stick closer to home, he deliberately allows French and 18th century influences to intrude too notably in several instances; yet practically all of his poems achieve consistent form. I think that its austerity and sense of timelessness make "Mountain

Valley" his best accomplished poem. Its intonation is suave and deeper than the graded accents of his other poems; its rhythm is accumulative of something less amiable, yet rarer and more abstract than his usual "Chaucerian" method of observation includes. Cowley seems to be civilized in the same sense as the older Chinamen. His alertness is a steady reassurance against crudities or bathos wherever his technical facilities may lead him.

John Brooks Wheelwright has little of Cowley's refinement, but the stertorous drive in several of his poems carries with it real emotional significance. The Hamilton poem, which best exemplifies this quality, is certainly one of the three best poems in the anthology, and the last verse of "Closing Gesture" is a statement so imaginative and balanced that it should be quoted:—

Myself,
stand against the black drift of storms,
trustful as the appealing brave, praying with his
    arms,
invincible as Hamilton in granite,
firm as a colossal crucifix upon a mountain trail
forever changeless against a changing sky.

It is good to find a poet with the power of fusing ideas with such subjective intensity that the result is poetry. Wheelwright's stringency is a rare quality in American poetry. We have had it in Robinson; but, unless I am mistaken, Wheelwright is emotionally more generously endowed, and, in spite of several second-rate poems, he offers interesting conjectures.

A detailed record of the Muses' bouts at Cambridge is included in Dorian Abbott's able preface. Turning poets loose is a natural privilege of universities, but it will never become, at least in our America, a popular inter-collegiate sport. The Fates are kind in this, even though the idea of the undergraduate anthology seldom gets as much encouragement as it really deserves.

[1923]

GENERAL AIMS AND THEORIES

When I started writing "Faustus & Helen" it was my intention to embody in modern terms (words, symbols, metaphors) a contemporary approximation to an ancient human culture or mythology that seems to have been obscured rather than illumined with the frequency of poetic allusions made to it during the last century. The name of Helen, for instance, has become an all-too-easily employed crutch for evocation whenever a poet felt a stitch in his side. The real evocation of this (to me) very real and absolute conception of beauty seemed to consist in a reconstruction in these modern terms of the basic emotional attitude toward beauty that the Greeks had. And in so doing I found that I was really building a bridge between so-called classic experience and many divergent realities of our seething, confused cosmos of today, which has no formulated mythology yet for classic poetic reference or for religious exploitation.

So I found "Helen" sitting in a street car; the Dionysian revels of her court and her seduction were transferred to a Metropolitan roof garden with a jazz orchestra; and the *katharsis* of the fall of Troy I saw approximated in the recent World War. The importance of this scaffolding may easily be exaggerated, but it gave me a series of correspondences between two widely separated worlds on which to sound some major themes of human speculation—love, beauty, death, renascence. It was a kind of grafting process that I shall doubtless not be interested in repeating, but which is consistent with subsequent theories of mine on the relation of tradition to the contemporary creating imagination.

It is a terrific problem that faces the poet today—a world that is so in transition from a decayed culture toward a reorganization of human evaluations that there are few common terms, general denominators of speech that are solid enough or that ring with any vibration or spiritual conviction. The great mythologies of the past (including the Church) are deprived of enough façade to even launch good raillery against. Yet much of their traditions are operative still—in millions of chance combinations of related and unrelated detail, psychological reference, figures of speech, precepts, etc. These are all a part of our common experience and the terms, at least partially, of that very experience when it defines or extends itself.

The deliberate program, then, of a "break" with the past or tradition seems to me to be a sentimental fallacy. . . . The poet has a right to draw on whatever practical resources he finds in books or otherwise about him. He must tax his sensibility and his touchstone of experience for the proper selections of these themes and details, however,—and that is where he either stands, or falls into useless archeology.

I put no particular value on the simple objective of "modernity." The element of the temporal location of an artist's creation is of very secondary importance; it can be left to the impressionist or historian just as well. It seems to me that a poet will accidentally define his time well enough simply by reacting honestly and to the full extent of his sensibilities to the states of passion, experience and rumination that fate forces on him, first hand. He must, of course, have a sufficiently universal basis of experience to make his imagination selective and valuable. His picture of the "period," then, will simply be a by-product of his curiosity and the relation of his experience to a postulated "eternity."

I am concerned with the future of America, but not because I think that America has any so-called par value as a state or as a group of people. . . . It is only because I feel persuaded that here are destined to be discovered certain as yet undefined spiritual quantities, perhaps a new hierarchy of faith not to be developed so completely elsewhere. And in this process I like to feel myself as a potential factor; certainly I must speak in its terms and what discoveries I may make are situated in its experience.

But to fool one's self that definitions are being reached by merely referring frequently to skyscrapers, radio antennae, steam whistles, or other surface phenomena of our time is merely to paint a photograph. I think that what is interesting and significant will emerge only under the conditions of our submission to, and examination and assimilation of the organic effects on us of these and other fundamental factors of our experience. It can certainly not be an organic expression otherwise. And the expression of such values may often be as well accomplished with the vocabulary and blank verse of the Elizabethans as with the calligraphic tricks and slang used so brilliantly at times by an impressionist like Cummings.

It may not be possible to say that there is, strictly speaking, any "absolute" experience. But it seems evident that certain aesthetic experience (and this may for a time engross the total faculties of the spectator) can be called absolute, inasmuch as it approximates a formally convincing statement of a conception or apprehension of life that gains our unquestioning assent, and under the conditions of which our imagination is unable to suggest a further detail consistent with the design of the aesthetic whole.

I have been called an "absolutist" in poetry, and if I am to welcome such a label it should be under the terms of the above definition. It is really only a *modus operandi*, however, and as such has been used organically before by at least a dozen poets such as Donne, Blake, Baudelaire, Rimbaud, etc. I may succeed in defining it better by contrasting it with the impressionistic method. The impressionist is interesting as far as he goes—but his goal has been reached when he has succeeded in projecting certain selected factual details into his reader's consciousness. He is really not interested in the *causes* (metaphysical) of his materials, their emotional derivations or their utmost spiritual consequences. A kind of retinal registration is enough, along with a certain psychological stimulation. And this is also true of your realist (of the Zola type), and to a certain extent of the classicist, like Horace, Ovid, Pope, etc.

Blake meant these differences when he wrote:

> We are led to believe in a lie
> When we see *with* not *through* the eye.

The impressionist creates only with the eye and for the readiest surface of the consciousness, at least relatively so. If the effect has been harmonious or even stimulating, he can stop there, relinquishing entirely to his audience the problematic synthesis of the details into terms of their own personal consciousness.

It is my hope to go *through* the combined materials of the poem, using our "real" world somewhat as a spring-board, and to give the poem *as a whole* an orbit or predetermined direction of its own. I would like to establish it as free from my own personality as from any chance evaluation on the reader's part. (This is, of course, an impossibility, but it is a characteristic worth mentioning.) Such a poem is at least a stab at a truth, and to such an extent may be differentiated from other kinds of poetry and called "absolute." Its evocation will not be toward decoration or amusement, but rather toward a state of consciousness, an "innocence" (Blake) or absolute beauty. In this condition there may be discoverable under new forms certain spiritual illuminations, shining with a morality essentialized from experience directly, and not from previous precepts or preconceptions. It is as though a poem gave the reader as he left it a single, new *word*, never before spoken and impossible to actually enunciate, but self-evident as an active principle in the reader's consciousness henceforward.

As to technical considerations: the motivation of the poem must be derived from the implicit emotional dynamics of the materials used, and the terms of expression employed are often selected less for their logical (literal) significance than for their associational meanings. Via this and their metaphorical inter-relationships, the entire construction of the poem is raised on the organic principle of a "logic of metaphor," which antedates our so-called pure logic, and which is the genetic basis of all speech, hence consciousness and thought-extension.

These dynamics often result, I'm told, in certain initial difficulties in understanding my poems. But on the other hand I find them at times the only means possible for expressing certain concepts in any forceful or direct way whatever. To cite two examples:—when, in "Voyages" (II), I speak of "adagios of islands," the reference is to the motion of a boat through islands clustered thickly, the rhythm of the motion, etc. And it seems a much more direct and creative statement than any more logical employment of words such as "coasting slowly through the islands," besides ushering in a whole world of music. Similarly in "Faustus and Helen" (III) the speed and tense altitude of an aeroplane are much better suggested by the idea of "nimble blue plateaus"—*implying* the aeroplane and its speed against a contrast of stationary elevated earth. Although the statement is pseudo in relation to formal logic—it *is* completely logical in relation to the truth of the imagination, and there is expressed a concept of speed and space that could not be handled so well in other terms.

In manipulating the more imponderable phenomena of psychic motives, pure emotional crystallizations, etc., I have had to rely even more on these dynamics of inferential mention, and I am doubtless still very unconscious of having committed myself to what seems nothing but obscurities to some minds. A poem like "Possessions" really cannot be technically explained. It must rely (even to a large extent with myself) on its organic impact on the imagination to successfully imply its meaning. This seems to me to present an exceptionally difficult problem, however, considering the real clarity and consistent logic of many of the other poems.

I know that I run the risk of much criticism by defending such theories as I have, but as it is part of a poet's business to risk not only criticism—but folly—in the conquest of consciousness I can only say that I attach no intrinsic value to what means I use beyond their practical service in giving form to the living stuff of the imagination.

New conditions of life germinate new forms of spiritual articulation. And while I feel that my work includes a more consistent extension of traditional literary elements than many contemporary poets are capable of appraising, I realize that I am utilizing the gifts of the past as instruments principally; and that the voice of the present, if it is to be known, must be caught at the risk of speaking in idioms and circumlocutions sometimes shocking to the scholar and historians of logic. Language has built towers and bridges, but itself is inevitably as fluid as always.

[1937]

A LETTER TO GORHAM MUNSON

Patterson, New York   *March 17, '26*

Dear Gorham: My rummy conversation last Monday offered, I fear, but a poor explanation of my several theoretical differences of opinion with you on the function of poetry, its particular province of activity, etc. Neither was I able to express to you my considerable appreciation of many accurate distinctions made in your essay which certainly prompt my gratitudes as well as applause. It would probably be uninteresting as well as a bit excessive for me to enumerate and dwell on these felicitations, however gratifying to myself I may feel them to be. Your essay is roughly divided in two, the second half including our present disagreement, and inasmuch as I have never really attempted to fulfill the functions therein attributed to the poet, your theories on that subject can be discussed from a relatively impersonal angle so far as I am concerned. Furthermore, it is *one* aspect of a contemporary problem which has already enlisted the most detailed and intense speculation from a number of fields, science, philosophy, etc., as you, of course, know. I'm not saying that my few hasty notes which follow are conclusive evidence, but the logic of them (added to the organic convictions incident to the memorized experience of the creative "act," let us say) is not yet sufficiently disproved for me by such arguments, at least, as you have used in your essay.

The editor wishes to acknowledge the University of California Press for selections from The Letters of Hart Crane, 1916–1932, *edited by Brom Weber, published in hardcover and paperback editions, 1965.*

Poetry, in so far as the metaphysics of any absolute knowledge extends, is simply the concrete *evidence* of the *experience* of a recognition (*knowledge* if you like). It can give you a *ratio* of fact and experience, and in this sense it is both perception and thing perceived, according as it approaches a significant articulation or not. This is its reality, its fact, *being*. When you attempt to ask more of poetry,—the fact of man's relationship to a hypothetical god, be it Osiris, Zeus, or Indra, you will get as variant terms even from the abstract terminology of philosophy as you will from poetry; whereas poetry, without attempting to logically enunciate such a problem or its solution, may well give you the real connective experience, the very "sign manifest" on which rests the assumption of a godhead.

I'm perfectly aware of my wholesale lack of knowledge. But as Allen said, what exactly do you mean by "knowledge"? When you ask for exact factual data (a graphic map of eternity?), ethical morality or moral classifications, etc., from poetry—you not only limit its goal, you ask its subordination to science, philosophy. Is it not equally logical to expect Stravinsky to bring his fiddles into dissent with the gravitation theories of Sir Isaac Newton? They *are* in dissent with this scientist, as a matter of fact, and organically so; for the group mind that Stravinsky appeals to has already been freed from certain of the limitations of experience and consciousness that dominated both the time and the mind of Newton. Science (ergo all exact knowledge and its instruments of operation) is in perfect antithesis to poetry. (Painting, architecture, music, as well.) It operates from an exactly opposite polarity, and it may equate with poetry, but when it does so its statement of such is in an entirely different terminology. I hope you get this difference between *inimical* and *antithetical*, intended here. It is not my interest

225

to discredit science, it has been as inspired as poetry, —and if you could but recognize it, much more hypothetically motivated.

What you admire in Plato as "divine sanity" is the architecture of his logic. Plato doesn't live today because of the intrinsic "truth" of his statements: their only living truth today consists in the "fact" of their harmonious relationship to each other in the context of his organization of them. This grace partakes of poetry. But Plato was primarily a philosopher, and you must admit that grace is a secondary motive in philosophical statement, at least until the hypothetical basis of an initial "truth" has been accepted—not in the name of beauty, form, or experience, but in the name of rationality. No wonder Plato considered the banishment of poets;—their reorganizations of chaos on basis perhaps divergent from his own threatened the logic of *his* system, itself founded on assumptions that demanded the very defense of poetic construction which he was fortunately able to provide.

The tragic quandary (or *agon*) of the modern world derives from the paradoxes that an inadequate system of rationality forces on the living consciousness. I am not opposing any new synthesis of reasonable laws which might provide a consistent philosophical and moral program for our epoch. Neither, on the other hand, am I attempting through poetry to delineate any such system. If this "knowledge," as you call it, were so sufficiently organized as to dominate the limitations of my personal experience (consciousness) then I would probably find myself automatically writing under its "classic" power of dictation, and under that circumstance might be incidentally as philosophically "contained" as you might wish me to be. That would mean "serenity" to you because the abstract basis of my work would have been familiarized to you before you read a word of the poetry. But my poetry, even then,—in so far as it was truly poetic,—would avoid the employment of abstract tags, formulations of experience in factual terms, etc.,—it would necessarily express its concepts in the more direct terms of physical-psychic experience. If not, it must by so much lose its impact and become simply categorical.

I think it must be due to some such misapprehensions of my poetic purpose in writing that leads you to several rather contradictory judgments which in one sentence are laudatory and in other contexts which you give them,—put me to blush for mental attitudes implied on my part. For instance, after having granted me all the praise you do earlier in your essay for "storming heaven" as it were, how can you later refer to that same faculty of verbal synchronization as to picture me as "waiting for another ecstasy"—and then "slumping"—rather as a baker would refer to a loaf in his oven. Granted your admiration for the "yeastiness" of some of my effusions, you should (in simple justice to your reader and your argument) here also afford the physical evidence (actual quotation or logical proof) of the "slump," the unleavened failure. There really are plenty of lines in this respect which could be used for illustration. What I'm objecting to is contained in my suspicion that you have allowed too many extra-literary impressions of me to enter your essay, sometimes for better, sometimes for worse. The same is true of your reference to the "psychological *gaming*" (Verlaine) which puts the slur of superficiality and vulgarity on the very aspects of my work which you have previously been at pains to praise.—And all because you arbitrarily propose a goal for me which I have no idea of nor interest in following. Either you find my work poetic or not, but if you propose for it such ends as poetry organically escapes, it seems to me, as Allen said, that you as a critic of literature are working into a confusion of categories. Certainly this charge of alternate "gutter sniping" and "angel kissing" is no longer anything more than a meretricious substitute for psychological sincerity in defining the range of an artist's subject matter and psychic explorations. Still less should it be brought forward unless there is enough physical evidence in the artist's work to warrant curiosity in this respect on the part of the reader.

Your difficulties are extra, I realize, in writing about me at all. They are bound to be thus extra because of the (so far as the reader goes) "impurities" of our previous literary arguments, intimacies of statement, semi-statements, etc., which are not always reflected in a man's work, after all. But your preoccupations on the one hand with a terminology which I have not attempted and your praise on the other hand of my actual (physical) representation of the incarnate *evidence* of the very knowledge, the very *wisdom* which you feel me to be only conjecturally sure of—makes me guilty of really wronging you, perhaps, but drives me to the platitude that "truth has no name." Her latest one, of course, is "relativity."

Apropos of all this the letter by Nichols in *The New Criterion* will interest you when you read it; there are interesting quotations from Goethe, Santayana, Russell, etc. And I am enclosing a hasty bundle of notes written at O'Neill's request for what angles they might suggest to him in writing a foreword for my book. (This, I hope, may be returned.)

Allen tells me that he has just mailed his note on me—for possible use in *The New Masses*. I told him to do this, not remembering definitely what you had told me about it before. It can do no harm anyway. I'm enclosing copies of the poems which Potamkin had intended using. It certainly was very kind of you to have suggested these matters to the *Masses* editor. Do let me hear from you soon.

PS—Needless to say, the notes for O'Neill contain repetitious matter for you, and certain accents were especially made against biases and critical deficiencies which I felt [might] lead to unwarranted assumptions, misplaced praises, etc., on his part. But the definitions of the "logic of metaphor," "dynamics of inferential mention," etc., I think are quite exact.

[1937]

A LETTER TO WALDO FRANK

[*Isle of Pines*]   *June 20th* [1926]

Dear Waldo: Recollection of certain statements made
in yesterday's letter to you prompt me to a little better
account of myself—not that I committed any insinceri-
ties (though the letter might seem to solicit sympathy
or encouragement) but that I feel guilty of an injustice
to you in some sort of way. You certainly do not deserve to have such fare set before you. . . .

So I apologize for my crudity, with the foreknowl-
edge of your understanding that there are times when
it is a torture to write anyone sincerely—as I must always write to you. My statements may appear in a less
insane light after you have read what has principally
spurred them—the Spengler thesis. This man is certainly fallible in plenty of ways but much of his
evidence is convincing—and is there any good evidence forthcoming from the world in general that the
artist isn't completely out of a job? Well, I may not care
about such considerations 2 hours from now, but at
present and for the last two months I have been con-
fronted with a ghostliness that is new.

The validity of a work of art is situated in contemporary reality to the extent that the artist must
honestly anticipate the realization of his vision in
"action" (as an actively operating principle of commu-
nal works and faith), and I don't mean by this that his
procedure requires any bona fide evidences directly
and personally signalled, nor even any physical signs
or portents. The darkness is part of his business. It has
always been taken for granted, however, that his intui-
tions were salutary and that his vision either sowed

or epitomized "experience" (in the Blakeian sense). Even the rapturous and explosive destructivism of Rimbaud presupposes this, even his lonely hauteur demands it for any estimation or appreciation. (The romantic attitude must at least have the background of an age of faith, whether approved or disproved no matter.)

All this is inconsecutive and indeterminate because I am trying to write shorthand about an endless subject—and moreover am unresolved as to any ultimate conviction. I am not fancying I am "enlightening" you about anything,—nor, if I thought I were merely exposing personal sores, would I continue to be so monotonous. Emotionally I should like to write *The Bridge*; intellectually judged the whole theme and project seems more and more absurd. A fear of personal impotence in this matter wouldn't affect me half so much as the convictions that arise from other sources. . . . I had what I thought were authentic materials that would have been a pleasurable-agony of wrestling, eventuating or not in perfection—at least being worthy of the most supreme efforts I could muster.

These "materials" were valid to me to the extent that I presumed them to be (articulate or not) at least organic and active factors in the experience and perceptions of our common race, time, and belief. The very idea of a bridge, of course, is a form peculiarly dependent on such spiritual convictions. It is an act of faith besides being a communication. The symbols of reality necessary to articulate the span—may not exist where you expected them, however. By which I mean that however great their subjective significance to me is concerned—these forms, materials, dynamics are simply non-existent in the world. I may amuse and delight and flatter myself as much as I please—but I am

231

only evading a recognition and playing Don Quixote in an immorally conscious way.

The form of my poem rises out of a past that so overwhelms the present with its worth and vision that I'm at a loss to explain my delusion that there exist any real links between that past and a future destiny worthy of it. The "destiny" is long since completed, perhaps the little last section of my poem is a hangover echo of it—but it hangs suspended somewhere in ether like an Absalom by his hair. The bridge as a symbol today has no significance beyond an economical approach to shorter hours, quicker lunches, behaviorism, and toothpicks. And inasmuch as the bridge is a symbol of all such poetry as I am interested in writing, it is my present fancy that a year from now I'll be more contented working in an office than before. Rimbaud was the last great poet that our civilization will see —he let off all the great cannon crackers in Valhalla's parapets, the sun has set theatrically several times since while Laforgue, Eliot, and others of that kidney have whimpered fastidiously. *Everybody* writes poetry now —and "poets" for the first time are about to receive official social and economic recognition in America. It's really all the fashion, but a dead bore to anticipate. If only America were half as worthy today to be spoken of as Whitman spoke of it fifty years ago there might be something for me to say—not that Whitman received or required any tangible proof of his intimations,. but that time has shown how increasingly lonely and ineffectual his confidence stands.

There always remains the cult of "words," elegancies, elaborations, to exhibit with a certain amount of pride to an "inner circle" of literary initiates. But this is, to me, rivalled by numerous other forms of social accomplishment which might, if attained, provide as mild and seductive recognitions. You probably think me completely insane, talking as obvious hysterics as [a] drunken chorus-girl. Well, perhaps I need a little more skepticism to put me right on *The Bridge* again. . . . I am certainly in a totally undignified mind and undress—and I hope to appear more solidly determined soon.

Please don't think that the O'Neill foreword has precipitated anything, nor that I [am] burning manuscripts or plotting oriental travels. . . . Desolately I confess that I *may* be writing stanzas again tomorrow. That's the worst of it. Mrs. S asks to be remembered to you.

—All this does not mean that I have resigned myself to inactivity. . . . A bridge will be written in some kind of style and form, at worst it will be something as good as advertising copy. After which I will have at least done my best to discharge my debt to Kahn's kindness.

[1952]

233

A LETTER TO HARRIET MONROE

Your good nature and manifest interest in writing me about the obscurities apparent in my Melville poem certainly prompt a wish to clarify my intentions in that poem as much as possible. But I realize that my explanations will not be very convincing. For a paraphrase is generally a poor substitute for any organized conception that one has fancied he has put into the more essentialized form of the poem itself.

At any rate, and though I imagine us to have considerable differences of opinion regarding the relationship of poetic metaphor to ordinary logic (I judge this from the angle of approach you use toward portions of the poem), I hope my answers will not be taken as a defense of merely certain faulty lines. I am really much more interested in certain theories of metaphor and technique involved generally in poetics, than I am concerned in vindicating any particular perpetrations of my own.

My poem may well be elliptical and actually obscure in the ordering of its content, but in your criticism of this very possible deficiency you have stated your objections in terms that allow me, at least for the moment, the privilege of claiming your ideas and ideals as theoretically, at least, quite outside the issues of my own aspirations. To put it more plainly, as a poet I may very possibly be more interested in the so-called illogical impingements of the connotations of words on the consciousness (and their combinations and interplay in metaphor on this basis) than I am interested in the preservation of their logically rigid significations at the cost of limiting my subject matter and perceptions involved in the poem.

This may sound as though I merely fancied juggling words and images until I found something novel, or esoteric; but the process is much more predetermined and objectified than that. The nuances of feeling and observation in a poem may well call for certain liberties which you claim the poet has no right to take. I am simply making the claim that the poet does have that authority, and that to deny it is to limit the scope of the medium so considerably as to outlaw some of the richest genius of the past.

This argument over the dynamics of metaphor promises as active a future as has been evinced in the past. Partaking so extensively as it does of the issues involved in the propriety or non-propriety of certain attitudes toward subject matter, etc., it enters the critical distinctions usually made between "romantic" [and] "classic" as an organic factor. It is a problem that would require many pages to state adequately—merely from my own limited standpoint on the issues. Even this limited statement may prove onerous reading, and I hope you will pardon me if my own interest in the matter carries me to the point of presumption.

Its paradox, of course, is that its apparent illogic operates so logically in conjunction with its context in the poem as to establish its claim to another logic, quite independent of the original definition of the word or phrase or image thus employed. It implies (this *inflection* of language) a previous or prepared receptivity to its stimulus on the part of the reader. The reader's sensibility simply responds by identifying this inflection of experience with some event in his own history or perceptions—or rejects it altogether. The logic of metaphor is so organically entrenched in pure sensibility that it can't be thoroughly traced or explained outside of historical sciences, like philology and anthropology. This "pseudo-statement," as I. A.

235

Richards calls it in an admirable essay touching our contentions in last July's *Criterion,* demands completely other faculties of recognition than the pure rationalistic associations permit. Much fine poetry may be completely rationalistic in its use of symbols, but there is much great poetry of another order which will yield the reader very little when inspected under the limitation of such arbitrary concerns as are manifested in your judgment of the Melville poem, especially when you constitute such requirements of ordinary logical relationship between word and word as irreducible.

I don't wish to enter here defense of the particular symbols employed in my own poem, because, as I said, I may well have failed to supply the necessary emotional connectives to the content featured. But I would like to counter a question or so of yours with a similar question. Here the poem is less dubious in quality than my own, and as far as the abstract pertinacity of question and its immediate consequences are concerned the point I'm arguing about can be better demonstrated. Both quotations are familiar to you, I'm sure.

You ask me how a *portent* can possibly be wound in a *shell.* Without attempting to answer this for the moment, I ask you how Blake could possibly say that "a *sigh* is a *sword* of an Angel King." You ask me how *compass, quadrant and sextant "contrive"* tides. I ask you how Eliot can possibly believe that "Every street *lamp* that I pass *beats* like a fatalistic *drum!*" Both of my metaphors may fall down completely. I'm not defending their actual value in themselves; but your criticism of them in each case was leveled at an illogicality of relationship between symbols, which similar fault you must have either overlooked in case you have ever admired the Blake and Eliot lines, or have there condoned them on account of some more ultimate convictions pressed on you by the impact of the poems in their entirety.

It all comes to the recognition that emotional dynamics are not to be confused with any absolute order of rationalized definitions; ergo, in poetry the *rationale* of metaphor belongs to another order of experience than science, and is not to be limited by a scientific and arbitrary code of relationships either in verbal inflections or concepts.

There are plenty of people who have never accumulated a sufficient series of reflections (and these of a rather special nature) to perceive the relation between a *drum* and a *street lamp*—*via* the *unmentioned* throbbing of the heart and nerves in a distraught man which *tacitly* creates the reason and "logic" of the Eliot metaphor. They will always have a perfect justification for ignoring those lines and to claim them obscure, excessive, etc., until by some experience of their own the words accumulate the necessary connotations to complete their connection. It is the same with the "patient etherized upon a table," isn't it? Surely that line must lack all eloquence to many people who, for instance, would delight in agreeing that the sky was like a dome of many-colored glass.

If one can't count on some such bases in the reader now and then, I don't see how the poet has any chance to ever get beyond the simplest conceptions of emotion and thought, of sensation and lyrical sequence. If the poet is to be held completely to the already evolved and exploited sequences of imagery and logic —what field of added consciousness and increased perceptions (the actual province of poetry, if not lullabies) can be expected when one has to relatively return to the alphabet every breath or so? In the minds of people who have sensitively read, seen, and experi-

237

enced a great deal, isn't there a terminology something like short-hand as compared to usual description and dialectics, which the artist ought to be right in trusting as a reasonable connective agent toward fresh concepts, more inclusive evaluations? The question is more important to me than it perhaps ought to be; but as long as poetry is written, an audience, however small, is implied, and there remains the question of an active or an inactive imagination as its characteristic.

It is of course understood that a street-lamp simply can't beat with a sound like a drum; but it often happens that images, themselves totally dissociated, when joined in the circuit of a particular emotion located with specific relation to both of them, conduce to great vividness and accuracy of statement in defining that emotion.

Not to rant on forever, I'll beg your indulgence and come at once to the explanations you requested on the Melville poem:

"The dice of drowned men's bones he saw bequeath
An embassy."

Dice bequeath an embassy, in the first place, by being ground (in this connection only, of course) in little cubes from the bones of drowned men by the action of the sea, and are finally thrown up on the sand, having "numbers" but no identification. These being the bones of dead men who never completed their voyage, it seems legitimate to refer to them as the only surviving evidence of certain messages undelivered, mute evidence of certain things, experiences that the dead mariners might have had to deliver. Dice as a symbol of chance and circumstance is also implied.

"The calyx of death's bounty giving back," etc.

This calyx refers in a double ironic sense both to a

cornucopia and the vortex made by a sinking vessel. As soon as the water has closed over a ship, this whirlpool sends up broken spars, wreckage, etc., which can be alluded to as livid *hieroglyphs*, making a *scattered chapter* so far as any complete record of the recent ship and her crew is concerned. In fact, about as much definite knowledge might come from all this as anyone might gain from the roar of his own veins, which is easily heard (haven't you ever done it?) by holding a shell close to one's ear.

"Frosted eyes lift altars."

Refers simply to a conviction that a man, not knowing perhaps a definite god yet being endowed with a reverence for deity—such a man naturally postulates a deity somehow, and the altar of that deity by the very *action* of the eyes *lifted* in searching.

"Compass, quadrant and sextant contrive no farther tides."

Hasn't it often occurred that instruments originally invented for record and computation have inadvertently so extended the concepts of the entity they were invented to measure (concepts of space, etc.) in the mind and imagination that employed them, that they may metaphorically be said to have extended the original boundaries of the entity measured? This little bit of "relativity" ought not to be discredited in poetry now that scientists are proceeding to measure the universe on principles of pure *ratio*, quite as metaphorical, so far as previous standards of scientific methods extended, as some of the axioms in Job.

I may have completely failed to provide any clear interpretation of these symbols in their context. And you will no doubt feel that I have rather heatedly explained them for anyone who professes no claims for

239

their particular value. I hope, at any rate, that I have clarified them enough to suppress any suspicion that their obscurity derives from a lack of definite intentions in the subject-matter of the poem. The execution is another matter, and you must be accorded a superior judgment to mine in that regard.

[1926]

A LETTER TO YVOR WINTERS

Patterson, New York   *May 29th, 1927*

Dear Winters: You need a good drubbing for all your
recent easy talk about "the complete man," the poet
and his ethical place in society, etc. I'm afraid I lack
the time right now to attempt what I might call a
relatively complete excuse for committing myself to
the above sentiments—and I am also encumbered by a
good deal of sympathy with your viewpoint in general. Wilson's article was just half-baked enough to
make one warm around the collar. It is so damned
easy for such as he, born into easy means, graduated
from a fashionable university into a critical chair over-
looking Washington Square, etc., to sit tight and hatch
little squibs of advice to poets not to be so "professional" as he claims they are, as though all the names
he has just mentioned had been as suavely nourished
as he—as though 4 out of 5 of them hadn't been
damned well forced the major part of their lives to
grub at *any* kind of work they could manage by hook or
crook and the fear of hell to secure! Yes, why not step
into the State Dept. and join the diplomatic corps for
a change! indeed, or some other courtly occupation
which would bring you into wide and active contact
with world affairs! As a matter of fact I'm all too ready
to concede that there are several other careers more
engaging to follow than that of poetry. But the circumstances of one's birth, the conduct of one's parents, the current economic structure of society, and a
thousand other local factors have as much or more to
say about successions to such occupations, the naive
volitions of the poet to the contrary. I agree with you,

241

of course, that the poet should in as large a measure as possible adjust himself to society. But the question always will remain as to how far the conscience is justified in compromising with the age's demands.

The image of "the complete man" is a good idealistic antidote for the hysteria for specialization that inhabits the modern world. And I strongly second your wish for some definite ethical order. Munson, however, and a number of my other friends, not so long ago, being stricken with the same urge, and feeling that something must be done about it—rushed into the portals of the famous Gurdjieff Institute and have since put themselves through all sorts of Hindu antics, songs, dances, incantations, psychic sessions, etc., so that now, presumably the left lobes of their brains and their right lobes respectively function (M's favorite word) in perfect unison. I spent hours at the typewriter trying to explain to certain of these urgent people why I could not enthuse about their methods; it was all to no avail, as I was told that the "complete man" had a different logic than mine, and further that there was no way of gaining or understanding this logic without first submitting yourself to the necessary training. I was finally left to roll in the gutter of my ancient predispositions, and suffered to receive a good deal of unnecessary pity for my obstinacy. Some of them, having found a good substitute for their former interest in writing by means of more complete formulas of expression, have ceased writing altogether, which is probably just as well. At any rate they have become hermetically sealed souls to my eyesight, and I am really not able to offer judgment.

I am not identifying your advice in any particular way with theirs, for you are certainly logical, so much so that I am inclined to doubt the success of your program even with yourself. Neither do you propose such paradoxical inducements as tea-dansants on Mt. Everest! I am only begging the question, after all, and asking you not to judge me too summarily by the shorthand statements that one has to use as the makeshift for the necessary chapters required for more explicit and final explanations. I am suspect, I fear, for equivocating. But I cannot flatter myself into quite as definite recipes for efficiency as you seem to, one reason being, I suppose, that I'm not so ardent an aspirant toward the rather classical characteristics that you cite as desirable. This is not to say that I don't "envy" the man who attains them, but rather that I have long since abandoned *that* field—and I doubt if I was born to achieve (with the particular vision) those richer syntheses of consciousness which we both agree in classing as supreme, at least the attitude of a Shakespeare or a Chaucer is not mine by organic rights, and why try to fool myself that I possess that type of vision when I obviously do not!

I have a certain code of ethics. I have not as yet attempted to reduce it to any exact formula, and if I did I should probably embark on an endless tome with monthly additions and digressions every year. It seems obvious that a certain decent carriage and action is a paramount requirement in any poet, deacon, or carpenter. And though I reserve myself the pleasant right to define these standards in a somewhat individual way, and to shout and complain when circumstances against me seem to warrant it, on the other hand I believe myself to be speaking honestly when I say that I have never been able to regret—for long—whatever has happened to me, more especially those decisions which at times have been permitted a free will. (Don't blame me entirely for bringing down all this simplicity on your head—your letter almost solicits it!) And I am as completely out of sympathy with the familiar whimpering caricature of the artist and his "divine rights" as you seem to be. I am not a Stoic, though I think I could lean more in that direction if I came to (as I may sometime) appreciate more highly the imaginative profits of such a course.

You put me in altogether too good company, you compliment me much too highly for me to offer the least resistance to your judgments on the structure of my work. I think I am quite unworthy of such associates as Marlowe or Valéry—except in some degree, perhaps, "by kind." If I can avoid the pearly gates long enough I may do better. Your fumigation of the Leonardo legend is a healthy enough reaction, but I don't think your reasons for doubting his intelligence and scope very potent. I've never closely studied the man's attainments or biography, but your argument is certainly weakly enough sustained on the sole prop of his sex—or lack of such. One doesn't have to turn to homosexuals to find instances of missing sensibilities. Of course I'm sick of all this talk about b——s and c——s in criticism. It's obvious that b——s are needed, and that Leonardo had 'em—at least the records of the Florentine prisons, I'm told, say so. You don't seem to realize that the whole topic is something of a myth anyway, and is consequently modified in the characteristics of the image by each age in each civilization. Tom Jones, a character for whom I have the utmost affection, represented the model in 18th century England, at least so far as the stated requirements in your letter would suggest, and for an Anglo-Saxon model he is still pretty good aside from calculus, the Darwinian theory, and a few other mental additions. Incidentally I think Tom Jones (Fielding himself, of course) represents a much more "balanced" attitude toward society and life in general than our friend, Thomas Hardy. Hardy's profundity is real, but it is voiced in pretty much one monotonous key. I think him perhaps the greatest technician in English verse since Shakespeare. He's a great poet and a mighty man. But you must be fanatic to feel that he fulfills the necessary "balanced ration" for modern consumption. Not one of his characters is for one moment allowed to express a single joyous passion without a forenote of Hardian doom entering the immediate description. Could Hardy create anything like Falstaff? I think that Yeats would be just as likely—more so.

That's what I'm getting at. . . . I don't care to be credited with too wholesale ambitions, for as I said, I realize my limitations, and have already partially furled my flag. The structural weaknesses which you find in my work are probably quite real, for I could not ask for a more meticulous and sensitive reader. It is my hope, of course, not only to improve my statement but to extend scope and viewpoint as much as possible. But I cannot trust to so methodical and predetermined a method of development, not by any means, as you recommend. Nor can I willingly permit you to preserve the assumption that I am seeking any "shortcuts across the circle," nor wilfully excluding any experience that seems to me significant. You seem to think that experience is some commodity—that can be sought! One can respond only to certain circumstances; just what the barriers are, and where the boundaries cross can never be completely known. And the surest way to frustrate the possibility of any free realization is, it seems to me, to wilfully direct it. I can't help it if you think me aimless and irresponsible. But try and see if you get such logical answers always from Nature as you seem to think you will! My "alert blindness" was a stupid ambiguity to use in any definition—but it seems to me you go in for just about as much "blind alertness" with some of your expectations.

If you knew how little of a metaphysician I am in the scholastic sense of the term, you would scarcely attribute such a conscious method to my poems (with regard to that element) as you do. I am an utter ignoramus in that whole subject, have never read Kant, Descartes, or other doctors. It's all an accident so far as my style goes. It happens that the first poem I ever wrote was too dense to be understood, and I now find that I can trust most critics to tell me that all my subsequent efforts have been equally futile. Having heard that one writes in a metaphysical vein, the usual critic will immediately close his eyes or stare with utter complacency at the page—assuming that black is black no more and that the poet means anything but what he says. It's as plain as day that I'm talking about war and aeroplanes in the passage from "F & H" ("corymbulous formations of mechanics," etc.) quoted by Wilson in *The New Republic*, yet by isolating these lines from the context and combining them suddenly with lines from a totally different poem he has the chance (and uses it) to make me sound like a perfect ninny. If I'd said that they were Fokker planes then maybe the critic would have had to notice the vitality of the metaphor and its pertinence. All this ranting seems somehow necessary. . . . If I am metaphysical I'm content to continue so. Since I have been "located" in this category by a number of people, I may as well go on alluding to certain (what are also called) metaphysical passages in Donne, Blake, Vaughan, etc., as being of particular appeal to me on a basis of common characteristics with what I like to do in my own poems, however little scientific knowledge of the subject I may have.

I write damned little because I am interested in recording certain sensations, very rigidly chosen, with an eye for what according to my taste and sum of prejudices seems suitable to—or intense enough—for verse. If I were writing in prose, as I sometime shall probably do, I should probably include a much thicker slice of myself—and though it is the height of conceit for me to suggest it, I venture to say that you may have received a somewhat limited idea of my interests and responses by judging me from my poems alone. I suppose that in regard to this limitation of poetic focus one should consult the current position of poetry in relation to other intellectual and political characteristics of the time, including a host of psychological factors which may or may not promote the fullest flowering of a particular medium such as verse. I am not apologizing. Nor am I trying to penetrate beyond a certain point into such labyrinths of conjecture and analysis. It seems unprofitable. One should be somewhat satisfied if one's work comes to approximate a true record of such moments of "illumination" as are occasionally possible. A sharpening of reality accessible to the poet, to no such degree possible through other mediums. That is one reason above all others—why I shall never expect (or indeed desire) *complete* sympathy from any writer of such originality as yourself. I may have neglected to say that I admire your general attitude, including your distrust of metaphysical or other patent methods. Watch out, though, that you don't strangulate yourself with some countermethod of your own!

[1937]

247

A LETTER TO OTTO H. KAHN

Patterson, New York   *September 12th, 1927*

Dear Mr. Kahn: I am taking for granted your continued interest in the progress of *The Bridge,* in which I
am still absorbed, and which has reached a stage where
its general outline is clearly evident. The Dedication
(recently published in *The Dial*) and Part I (now in
The American Caravan) you have already seen, but as
you may not have them presently at hand I am including them in a ms. of the whole, to date, which I am
sending you under separate cover.

At the risk of complicating your appreciation of Part
II ("Powhatan's Daughter"), I nevertheless feel im-
pelled to mention a few of my deliberate intentions in
this part of the poem, and to give some description of
my general method of construction. Powhatan's daughter, or Pocahontas, is the mythological nature-symbol
chosen to represent the physical body of the continent,
or the soil. She here takes on much the same role as
the traditional Hertha of ancient Teutonic mythology.
The five sub-sections of Part II are mainly concerned
with a gradual exploration of this "body" whose first
possessor was the Indian. It seemed altogether ineffec-
tive from the poetic standpoint to approach this material from the purely chronological angle—beginning
with, say, the landing of "The Mayflower," continuing
with a résumé of the Revolution through the conquest
of the West, etc. One can get that viewpoint in any
history primer. What I am after is an assimilation of
this experience, a more organic panorama, showing the
continuous and living evidence of the past in the inmost vital substance of the present.

Consequently I jump from the monologue of Co-

lumbus in "Ave Maria"—right across the four intervening centuries—into the harbor of 20th-century Manhattan. And from that point in time and place I begin
to work backward through the pioneer period, always
in terms of the present—finally to the very core of the
nature-world of the Indian. What I am really handling,
you see, is the Myth of America. Thousands of strands
have had to be searched for, sorted, and interwoven.
In a sense I have had to do a great deal of pioneering
myself. It has taken a great deal of energy—which has
not been so difficult to summon as the necessary patience to wait, simply wait much of the time—until my
instincts assured me that I had assembled my materials
in proper order for a final welding into their natural
form. For each section of the entire poem has presented its own unique problem of form, not alone in
relation to the materials embodied within its separate
confines, but also in relation to the other parts, *in series*, of the major design of the entire poem. Each is a
separate canvas, as it were, yet none yields its entire
significance when seen apart from the others. One
might take the Sistine Chapel as an analogy. It might
be better to read the following notes *after* rather than
before your reading of the ms. They are not necessary
for an understanding of the poem, but I think they
may prove interesting to you as a commentary on my
architectural method.

1. "The Harbor Dawn":

Here the movement of the verse is in considerable
contrast to that of the "Ave Maria," with its sea-swell
crescendo and the climacteric vision of Columbus.
This legato, in which images blur as objects only half
apprehended on the border of sleep and consciousness,
makes an admirable transition between the intervening centuries.

The love-motif (in italics) carries along a symbolism

of the life and ages of man (here the sowing of the seed) which is further developed in each of the subsequent sections of "Powhatan's Daughter," though it is never particularly stressed. In 2 ("Van Winkle") it is Childhood; in 3 it is Youth; in 4, Manhood; in 5 it is Age. This motif is interwoven and tends to be implicit in the imagery rather than anywhere stressed.

2. "Van Winkle":

The protagonist has left the room with its harbor sounds, and is walking to the subway. The rhythm is quickened; it is a transition between sleep and the immanent tasks of the day. Space is filled with the music of a hand organ and fresh sunlight, and one has the impression of the whole continent—from Atlantic to Pacific—freshly arisen and moving. The walk to the subway arouses reminiscences of childhood, also the "childhood" of the continental conquest, viz., the conquistadores, Priscilla, Capt. John Smith, etc. These parallelisms unite in the figure of Rip Van Winkle who finally becomes identified with the protagonist, as you will notice, and who really boards the subway with the reader. He becomes the "guardian angel" of the journey into the past.

3. "The River":

The subway is simply a figurative, psychological "vehicle" for transporting the reader to the Middle West. He lands on the railroad tracks in the company of several tramps in the twilight. The extravagance of the first twenty-three lines of this section is an intentional burlesque on the cultural confusion of the present—a great conglomeration of noises analogous to the strident impression of a fast express rushing by. The rhythm is jazz.

Thenceforward the rhythm settles down to a steady pedestrian gait, like that of wanderers plodding along. My tramps are psychological vehicles, also. Their wanderings, as you will notice, carry the reader into interior after interior, finally to the great River. They are the left-overs of the pioneers in at least this respect—that their wanderings carry the reader through an experience parallel to that of Boone and others. I think [I] have caught some of the essential spirit of the Great Valley here, and in the process have approached the primal world of the Indian, which emerges with a full orchestra in the succeeding dance.

5[4]. "The Dance":

Here one is on the pure mythical and smoky soil at last! Not only do I describe the conflict between the two races in this dance—I also become identified with the Indian and his world before it is over, which is the only method possible of ever really possessing the Indian and his world as a cultural factor. I think I really succeed in getting under the skin of this glorious and dying animal, in terms of expression, in symbols, which he himself would comprehend. Pocahontas (the continent) is the common basis of our meeting, she survives the extinction of the Indian, who finally, after being assumed into the elements of nature (as he understood them), persists only as a kind of "eye" in the sky, or as a star that hangs between day and night—"the twilight's dim perpetual throne."

6[5]. "Indiana":

I regret that this section is not completed as yet. It will be the monologue of an Indiana farmer; time, about 1860. He has failed in the gold-rush and is returned to till the soil. His monologue is a farewell to his son, who is leaving for a life on the sea. It is a lyrical summary of the period of conquest, and his wife, the mother who died on the way back from the gold-rush, is alluded to in a way which implies her succession to the nature-symbolism of Pocahontas. I have this section well-nigh done, but there is no use including [it] in the present ms. without the final words.

The next section, "Cutty Sark," is a phantasy on the period of the whalers and clipper ships. It also starts in the present and "progresses backwards." The form of the poem may seem erratic, but it is meant to present the hallucinations incident to rum-drinking in a South Street dive, as well as the lurch of a boat in heavy seas, etc. So I allow myself something of the same freedom which E. E. Cummings often uses.

"Cutty Sark" is built on the plan of a *fugue*. Two "voices"—that of the world of Time, and that of the world of Eternity—are interwoven in the action. The Atlantis theme (that of Eternity) is the transmuted voice of the nickel-slot pianola, and this voice alternates with that of the derelict sailor and the description of the action. The airy regatta of phantom clipper ships seen from Brooklyn Bridge on the way home is quite effective, I think. It was a pleasure to use historical names for these lovely ghosts. Music still haunts their names long after the wind has left their sails.

"Cape Hatteras," which follows, is unfinished. It will be a kind of ode to Whitman. I am working as much as possible on it now. It presents very formidable problems, as, indeed, all the sections have. I am really writing an epic of the modern consciousness, and indescribably complicated factors have to be resolved and blended. . . . I don't wish to tire you [with] too extended an analysis of my work, and so shall leave the other completed sections to explain themselves. In the ms., where the remaining incompleted sections occur, I am including a rough synopsis of their respective themes, however. The range of *The Bridge* has been called colossal by more than one critic who has seen the ms. And though I have found the subject to be vaster than I had at first realized, I am still highly confident of its final articulation into a continuous and eloquent span. Already there are evident signs of recognition: the following magazines have taken various sections:

"Dedication: To Brooklyn Bridge"	*The Dial*
"Ave Maria"	*The American Caravan*
"The Harbor Dawn"	*transition* (Paris)
"Van Winkle"	"
"The River"	*The Virginia Quarterly*
"The Dance"	*The Dial*
"Cutty Sark"	*Poetry* (Chicago)
"Three Songs"	*The Calendar* (London)
"The Tunnel"	*The Criterion* (London)

(I have been especially gratified by the reception accorded me by *The Criterion*, whose director, Mr. T. S. Eliot, is representative of the most exacting literary standards of our times.)

For some time past I have been seeking employment in New York, but without success so far. It's the usual problem of mechanical prejudices that I've already grown grey in trying to deal with. But all the more difficult now, since the only references I can give for the last two years are my own typewriter and a collection of poems. I am, as you will probably recall, at least avowedly—a perfectly good advertising writer. I am wondering if you would possibly give me some recommendation to the publicity department of The Metropolitan Opera Company, where I am certain of making myself useful. I was in New York two days last week, trying to secure employment as a waiter on one of the American lines. I found that I needed something like a diploma from Annapolis before hoping for an interview. A few years ago I registered with the Munson Line with reference to my qualifications for a particular position which every ship includes—that of "ship's writer," or "deck yeoman"; but I always found that such jobs were dispensed to acquaintances of the captain or to office workers, and that my references were never taken from the file. I am not particular what I do, however, so long as there is reasonable chance of my doing it well, and any recommendation you might care to offer in any practical direction whatever will be most welcome. My present worried state of mind practically forbids any progress on *The Bridge*, the chances for which are considerably better under even greatly limited time conditions.

I am still assured of a definite inheritance, previously mentioned in my first letter to you; and if you care to consider advancing me, say 800 or 1,000 dollars, on the same basis of insurance security as your previous assistance, I should be glad to come into New York and talk it over. There is no monetary standard of evaluation for works of art, I know, but I cannot help feeling that a great poem may well be worth at least the expenditure necessary for merely the scenery and costumes of many a flashy and ephemeral play, or for a motor car. The *Aeneid* was not written in two years—nor in four, and in more than one sense I feel justified in comparing the historic and cultural scope of *The Bridge* to this great work. It is at least a symphony with an epic theme, and a work of considerable profundity and inspiration. Even with the torturing heat of my sojourn in Cuba I was able to work faster than before or since then, in America. The "foreignness" of my surroundings stimulated me to the realization of natively American materials and viewpoints in myself not hitherto suspected, and in one month I was able to do more work than I had done in the three previous years. If I could work in Mexico or Mallorca this winter I could have *The Bridge* finished by next spring. But that is a speculation which depends entirely on your interest.

Please pardon the inordinate length of this letter. I shall, of course, hope to hear from you regarding your impressions of the poem as it now stands. Along with the ms., I am enclosing three critical articles which may interest you somewhat.

[1937]

255

A LETTER TO HERBERT WEINSTOCK

Patterson, New York   *April 22nd, 1930*

Dear Herbert Weinstock: You have my sincerest gratitude for your enthusiastic review of *The Bridge*. Van Vuren had already sent me a copy, and I was just on the point of writing you my thanks when along came your good letter.

I hope I am deserving of such lofty companions as you group me with. I am almost tempted to believe your claims on the strength of your amazing insight into my objectives in writing, my particular symbolism, the intentional condensation and "density" of structure that I occasionally achieve, and the essential religious motive throughout my work. This last-mentioned feature commits me to self-consciousness on a score that makes me belie myself a little. For I have never consciously approached any subject in a religious mood; it is only afterward that I, or someone else generally, have noticed a prevalent piety. God save me from a Messianic predisposition!

It is pertinent to suggest, I think, that with more time and familiarity with *The Bridge* you will come to envisage it more as one poem with a clearer and more integrated unity and development than was at first evident. At least if my own experience in reading and rereading Eliot's *Wasteland* has any relation to the circumstances this *may* be found to be the case. It took me nearly five years, with innumerable readings, to convince myself of the essential unity of that poem. And *The Bridge* is at least as complicated in its structure and inferences as *The Wasteland*—perhaps more so.

[1952]

A LETTER TO ALLEN TATE

Gaylordsville, Conn.   *July 13th, 1930*

Dear Allen: Your last good letter and the admirable review of *The Bridge* in *The Hound & Horn* deserved an earlier response, but time has somehow just been drifting by without my being very conscious of it. For one thing, I have been intending to get hold of a copy of *The Hound & Horn* and give your review a better reading, before replying, than I could achieve at the tables in Brentano's when I was in town about two weeks ago. I still haven't a copy and consequently may wrong you in making any comments whatever. But as I don't want to delay longer I hope you'll pardon any discrepancies.

The fact that you posit *The Bridge* at the end of a tradition of romanticism may prove to have been an accurate prophecy, but I don't yet feel that such a statement can be taken as a foregone conclusion. A great deal of romanticism may persist—of the sort to deserve serious consideration, I mean.

But granting your accuracy—I shall be humbly grateful if *The Bridge* can fulfil simply the metaphorical inferences of its title. . . . You will admit our age (at least our predicament) to be one of transition. If *The Bridge*, embodying as many anomalies as you find in it, yet contains as much authentic poetry here and there as even Winters grants,—then perhaps it can serve as at least the function of a link connecting certain chains of the past to certain chains and tendencies of the future. In other words, a diagram or "process" in the sense that Genevieve Taggard refers to all my work in estimating Kunitz's achievement in the enclosed review. This gives it no more interest than as a point of chronological reference, but "nothing ventured, nothing gained"—and I can't help thinking that my mistakes may warn others who may later be tempted to an interest in similar subject matter.

Personally I think that Taggard is a little too peremptory in dispensing with Kunitz's "predecessors." We're all unconscious evolutionists, I suppose, but she apparently belongs to the more rabid ranks. I can't help wishing I had read more of Kunitz before seeing her review. He is evidently an excellent poet. I should like to have approached him, not as one bowing before Confucius, nor as one buying a new nostrum for lame joints. Taggard, like Winters, isn't looking for poetry any more. Like Munson, they are both in pursuit of some cure-all. Poetry as poetry (and I don't mean merely decorative verse) isn't worth a second reading any more. Therefore—away with Kubla Khan, out with Marlowe, and to hell with Keats! It's a pity, I think. So many true things have a way of coming out all the better without the strain to sum up the universe in one impressive little pellet. I admit that I don't answer the requirements. My vision of poetry *is* too personal to "answer the call." And if I ever write any more verse it will probably be at least as personal as the idiom of *White Buildings* whether anyone cares to look at it or not.

This personal note is doubtless responsible for what you term as sentimentality in my attitude toward Whitman.* It's true that my rhapsodic address to him in *The Bridge* exceeds any exact evaluation of the man. I realized that in the midst of the composition. But since you and I hold such divergent prejudices regarding the value of the materials and events that W. responded to, and especially as you, like so many others,

* In a letter to Crane, June 10, 1930.

never seem to have read his *Democratic Vistas* and other of his statements sharply decrying the materialism, industrialism, etc., of which you name him the guilty and hysterical spokesman, there isn't much use in my tabulating the qualified, yet persistent reasons I have for my admiration of him, and my allegiance to the positive and universal tendencies implicit in nearly all his best work. You've heard me roar at too many of his lines to doubt that I can spot his worst, I'm sure.

It amuses me to see how Taggard takes up some of Winters' claims against me (I expected this and look for more) in his article in the Anti-Humanist volume, especially as that borrowing doesn't seem to have obviated his own eclipse according to her estimate of the new constellation. I have the feeling that Miss Taggard is not only conducting her own education in public (as someone once said of George Moore) but also the education of her subjects. . . . At least she seems now to have attained that acumen which is a confusion to all.

[1937]

259

MODERN POETRY

Modern poetry has long since passed the crest of its rebellion against many of the so-called classical strictures. Indeed the primary departures of the early intransigeants were often more in a classic direction, with respect to certain neglected early European traditions, than were many of the Victorian regulations that formed the immediate butt of attack.

Revolution flourishes still, but rather as a contemporary tradition in which the original obstacles to freedom have been, if not always eradicated, at least obscured by floods of later experimentation. Indeed, to the serious artist, revolution as an all-engrossing program no longer exists. It persists at a rapid momentum in certain groups or movements, but often in forms which are more constricting than liberating, in view of a generous choice of subject matter.

The poet's concern must be, as always, self-discipline toward a formal integration of experience. For poetry is an architectural art, based not on Evolution or the idea of progress, but on the articulation of the contemporary human consciousness *sub specie æternitatis,* and inclusive of all readjustments incident to science and other shifting factors related to that consciousness. The key to the process of free creative activity which Coleridge gave us in his *Lectures on Shakespeare* exposes the responsibilities of every poet, modern or ancient, and cannot be improved upon. "No work of true genius," he says, "dares want its appropriate form, neither indeed is there any danger of this. As it must not, so genius can not, be lawless: for it is even this that constitutes its genius—*the power of acting creatively under laws of its own origination.*"

Poetry has at once a greater intimacy and a wider, more exact scope of implication than painting or any of the other arts. It is therefore more apt to be indicative of impending changes in other media such as painting or music. This is a logical deduction that facts do not always favor, as in the case of some modern composers such as Stravinsky, the full purport of whose inspiration seems to lie beyond the reach of current literary expression. Literature has a more tangible relationship to painting; and it is highly probable that the Symbolist movement in French poetry was a considerable factor in the instigation first, of Impressionism, and later, of Cubism. Both arts have had parallel and somewhat analogous tendencies toward abstract statement and metaphysical representation. In this recent preoccupation it is certain that both media were responding to the shifting emphasis of the Western World away from religion toward science. Analysis and discovery, the two basic concerns of science, became conscious objectives of both painter and poet. A great deal of modern painting is as independent of any representational motive as a mathematical equation; while some of the most intense and eloquent current verse derives sheerly from acute psychological analysis, quite independent of any dramatic motivation.

The function of poetry in a Machine Age is identical to its function in any other age; and its capacities for presenting the most complete synthesis of human values remain essentially immune from any of the so-called inroads of science. The emotional stimulus of machinery is on an entirely different psychic plane from that of poetry. Its only menace lies in its capacities for facile entertainment, so easily accessible as to arrest the development of any but the most negligible esthetic responses. The ultimate influence of machinery in this respect remains to be seen, but its firm entrenchment in our lives has already produced a series of challenging new responsibilities for the poet.

For unless poetry can absorb the machine, i.e., *ac-*

climatize it as naturally and casually as trees, cattle, galleons, castles and all other human associations of the past, then poetry has failed of its full contemporary function. This process does not infer any program of lyrical pandering to the taste of those obsessed by the importance of machinery; nor does it essentially involve even the specific mention of a single mechanical contrivance. It demands, however, along with the traditional qualifications of the poet, an extraordinary capacity for surrender, at least temporarily, to the sensations of urban life. This presupposes, of course, that the poet possesses sufficient spontaneity and gusto to convert this experience into positive terms. Machinery will tend to lose its sensational glamour and appear in its true subsidiary order in human life as use and continual poetic allusion subdue its novelty. For, contrary to general prejudice, the wonderment experienced in watching nose dives is of less immediate creative promise to poetry than the familiar gesture of a motorist in the modest act of shifting gears. I mean to say that mere romantic speculation on the power and beauty of machinery keeps it at a continual remove; it can not act creatively in our lives until, like the unconscious nervous responses of our bodies, its connotations emanate from within—forming as spontaneous a terminology of poetic reference as the bucolic world of pasture, plow, and barn.

The familiar contention that science is inimical to poetry is no more tenable than the kindred notion that theology has been proverbially hostile—with the *Commedia* of Dante to prove the contrary. That "truth" which science pursues is radically different from the metaphorical, extra-logical "truth" of the poet. When Blake wrote that "a tear is an intellectual thing, And a sigh is the sword of an Angel King"—he was not in any logical conflict with the principles of the Newtonian Universe. Similarly, poetic prophecy in the case of the seer has nothing to do with factual prediction or with futurity. It is a peculiar type of perception, capable of apprehending some absolute and timeless concept of the imagination with astounding clarity and conviction.

That the modern poet can profitably assume the roles of philosopher or theologian is questionable at best. Science, the uncanonized Deity of the times, seems to have automatically displaced the hierarchies of both Academy and Church. It is pertinent to cite the authors of the *Commedia* and *Paradise Lost* as poets whose verse survives the religious dogmas and philosophies of their respective periods, but it is fallacious to assume that either of these poets could have written important religious verse without the fully developed and articulated religious dogmas that each was heir to.

The future of American poetry is too complicated a speculation to be more than approached in this limited space. Involved in it are the host of considerations relative to the comparative influences of science, machinery, and other factors which I have merely touched upon;—besides those influential traditions of early English prosody which form points of departure, at least, for any indigenous rhythms and forms which may emerge. The most typical and valid expression of the American *psychosis* seems to me still to be found in Whitman. His faults as a technician and his clumsy and indiscriminate enthusiasm are somewhat beside the point. He, better than any other, was able to coördinate those forces in America which seem most intractable, fusing them into a universal vision which takes on additional significance as time goes on. He was a revolutionist beyond the strict meaning of Coleridge's definition of genius, but his bequest is still to be realized in all its implications.   [1930]

FROM HAUNTS OF PROSERPINE

To write adequate biography is one task, but to convey that record convincingly in terms of heroic couplets is a far more delicate achievement. It involves a closer identification of the author with the intimate aspirations of his subject—an even finer apprehension of his very pulse and successive subconscious motivations than most matter-of-fact accounts take into consideration. James Whaler, inspired by the noble vision and tragic frustrations of the Sicilian-American naturalist, Constantine Rafinesque, has taken a life that is all but forgotten, and so illumined it with the intrinsic light of its own Shelleyan pantheism and purity of motive that this long dramatic monologue, in which the aging botanist pours out his recollections, penetrates and transcends the bare recorded facts of his career. And if this results in a characterization imposing enough to take on some of the outlines of a myth, it is all to Mr. Whaler's credit as a poet. In so doing he has been but the more faithful to his subject, whose scientific obsessions were the active manifestations of a poetic imagination.

A beautiful and adulterous wife robbed Rafinesque of his native Sicily and all further hope of earthly love. His courtship of this daughter of a Greek innkeeper, his subsequent struggle between the claims of science and matrimony, and his desperate and lonely departure for the unpoisoned wildernesses of the New World form the theme of the first half of *Green River*. But still more disastrous was the storm which foundered his ship in Long Island Sound, swallowing within call of shore his fifty boxes of scientific equipment [and] his books, manuscripts and funds, the results of years of devoted labor. Later on, while working in a Philadelphia counting-house, he was to hear how his wife—whom he constantly envisages as "Proserpine"—was squandering what remained of his once ample fortune in frolic with an island lover. But the final blow came with the death of John Clifford, his friend and benefactor, for whose sake he had gone west into Kentucky.

It is easy to conceive how this series of calamities could confuse the vision of the staunchest spirit. Rafinesque died, a half-insane pauper in a garret on lower Race Street, Philadelphia, in 1840. During his twenty-five years in America, however, he had been a lecturer —received and remembered with honor—at Transylvania University; had crossed the Alleghanies five times on foot rather than by horse, in order to neglect no possible discoveries of uncharted forms of natural life; and had consistently held the respect, if not always the unbiased understanding, of Audubon and other more fortunate representative scientists of his period. The cave region along the Green River in Kentucky still has mementoes of his wanderings; and it is in his monologue relating his presumable discovery of what is actually named Rafinesque's Cave that his high moral conscience and lyric phantasy unite in a scene (*Section II*) which forms the poem's dramatic apex. There, amidst "Babylons of stalactite"—

Where pearl-boughs blossoming in bursts of stars
Show me a jeweled heaven of dead czars,
And moon-tailed orioles roost wing to wing
With mocking-birds that only dream they sing—

as this nacreous Plutonian palace unfolds before him, his ecstasy conceives an idealistic prehistoric race of river-men about him, stone-frozen, "paired lovers all, in a dominion where beauty is omnipotent with

265

death." Before him also looms the mummy-phantasy of his wife, his "Proserpine" of bitter memory, whose beautiful image he there commits to flames, burning her imprint forever from his heart.

The curtain falls on Rafinesque before the tragic breakup of his faculties, but already in his Race Street garret over-looking the shipping on the Delaware. In a stoic refrain he is left in contemplation of the world about him:

> With masts and mariners before
> Your window, street-cries in your ears,
> There lay your bed, there nail your desk,
> There leaven all you know with tears.

Green River contains few of those psychological nuances and moral casuistries abounding in the narrative verse of Mr. Robinson, Mr. Aiken, and others. Though it often features nature, society, and the individual at odds, they are like the more elemental odds that have occupied such themes as Masefield's. *Green River* is often melodramatic with expletives, rhapsodic flights of fancy, and bitter invocations. Perhaps any extended monologue must be so rhetorically energized in order to sustain the burden of so long a narrative. But here one occasionally feels a strain in the otherwise vigorous and tough texture of the verse, so felicitously inlaid with a thousand names from field and stream. Rafinesque speaks in this multitudinous world of flowers, birds, and fish as intensely as an astronomer breathes among the stars. Mr. Whaler's fresh evocation of this natural background (so prettified and sterile in most hands) is almost as fine an achievement as his resurrection of a forgotten hero.

[1932]

APPENDIX

Hart Crane, by Waldo Frank

HART CRANE

There is a tradition in our land old as Roger Williams and the Pilgrims. It takes the term *New World* with literal seriousness. America, it declares, shall be the New Jerusalem, the kingdom of Heaven brought from within each man to earth, and expressed in the forms of our American society. The deepest aesthetic creators of America have been partisans, indeed hierophants, of this tradition. It is implicit in Emerson's social criticism (although his transcendentalism opposes it). It inspired the anti-transcendentalism, the civil disobedience of Thoreau. It is in Emily Dickinson's hermetic little poems, as the flower is in the bud. It explains the despair of Melville's hunting the White Whale; it is the motive (this is less understood) of Poe's metaphysical concern. And of course Walt Whitman is its major prophet, not only in his apocalyptic poems but in the fierce social and cultural criticism of *Democratic Vistas*, in which America is excoriated for not living up to the prophet's program for a republic of brothers. Hart Crane is the poet of our recent time who most consciously inherits this tradition, and most superbly carries it on.

America has more popular literary traditions. There is the mystical withdrawal and escape, abandoning this world to damnation, implicit in Hawthorne, melodiously explicit in T. S. Eliot. Most prevalent of all, there is the tradition of our realists, our rationalists, whose literary quality ranges from the crass stuff of James Fenimore Cooper, the mild anodyne of Washington Irving, to the lace and filigree of Henry James.

Indeed, the great tradition, with its demand that men, here on earth, within an American social structure, work out the revelation of God, is often present only as a river flowing underground, nourishing but unseen. Whitman's challenge was not widely accepted; the plain-minded folk, the fact-minded poets of his time and ours resisted him. Hart Crane shares Whitman's fate. The majority of his fellow citizens prefer to conceive of the Brooklyn Bridge as a passage made of iron from one borough to another rather than as the mythic symbol of how man *in his works* shall immanentize and realize revelation. But like the mystic "Song of Myself," Crane's poems have the indestructibility of their deep vision of man's ultimate nature.

Whitman's prosody was the composition of the current trends—literary, ideological, political, of the period roughly 1850–70. The texture of Crane's writing is the fruit of a far more sophisticated era. The readings of the Elizabethans, of Melville, of the Symbolists of France wrought an idiom for Crane which is quite distinct from the idiom of Whitman—as New York of 1920 is distinct from the "barbaric yawp" of Mannahatta. Crane was not an epigone of Whitman; he was a creative continuator of the basic theme, in Whitman, of man's transfiguration. Great traditions are extended not by imitators but by original transformers.

For Whitman, the founding of Zion in America meant the experience of the Scriptures applied to the crowds on his Broadway, to the prairie and the Open Road. To Crane, it meant these also, but in the jungle of the Machine, in the airs of jazz, in the matrix of skyscraper and of subway.

The mystic is a man who *knows* by immediate experience the organic continuity between his self and the cosmos. (The intellectual conviction may come later; the belief in God may not come at all.) Whitman's "immediate experience" embraced an America still simple enough for his daily life to absorb it. Crane inherited a jungle of machines and disintegrating values which he had no discipline or method to manage and which soon destroyed him.

Harold Hart Crane was born in Garrettsville, Ohio, July 21, 1899. His parents, Clarence Arthur Crane and Grace Hart, were of the pioneer stock that trekked in covered wagons from New England to the Western Reserve. But his grandparents on both sides had already shifted from farm to city life; and Clarence Crane became a wealthy candy manufacturer in Cleveland. Here, the poet, an only child, lived from his tenth year. At thirteen he was composing verse. In the winter of 1916 he went with his mother, who had separated from his father, to the Isle of Pines, south of Cuba, where his grandfather Hart had a fruit ranch; and this journey, which gave him his first experience of the sea, was cardinal in his growth. The following year he was in New York; in contact with *The Little Review* of Margaret Anderson and Jane Heap; tutoring for college; already passionately and rather wildly living.

At this time two mutually exclusive trends divided the American literary scene. One was centered in Ezra Pound, Alfred Kreymborg, the Imagists, Harriet Monroe's *Poetry*, and *The Little Review*; the other was grouped around *The Seven Arts*. Young Crane was in vital touch with both. He was reading Marlowe, Donne, Rimbaud, Laforgue; but he was also exploring American life in Whitman, Sherwood Anderson, and Melville. His action, when America entered the war, reveals the complexity of his interests. He gave up college and by his own choice returned to Cleveland to work as a common laborer in a munitions plant and a shipyard. He loved machines, the earth-tang of the workers. But he also loved music; he wanted to write, to meditate, to read. The conflict of desires led him perhaps to accept what seemed a comfortable compromise: a job in the factory of his father, where he hoped to find some leisure without losing contact with the industrial world.

The elder Crane, a man of turbulent and twisted power, was outraged by the jest of fortune that had given him a poet for a son. He set to work to "drive the poetry nonsense" out of his boy's mind. When in 1920 Hart broke with both Cleveland and his father, the exquisite balance of his nerves was already permanently impaired.

The important poems of *White Buildings*, his first volume, reveal the sea as the symbol of Crane's integration. And the sea means regression, human surrender. In 1924, Crane was living at Columbia Heights, Brooklyn, in range of the harbor, the bridge, the sea sounds. Now a new and positive theme came to him: one that was both cosmic and human. Before the close of 1925, he had achieved the pattern of his major poem. Only later did Crane learn that the house where the vision of *The Bridge* first came to him, and where he finished it, had been the property of Washington Roebling, the paralyzed engineer of Brooklyn Bridge, and that the very room where Crane lived and wrote had been used by Roebling as an observation tower to watch the bridge's construction.

The Bridge was published early in 1930. Crane went to Mexico: his plan being to write a poem on the history of Montezuma, a variation on the positive theme which *The Bridge* stated.

The principle that Crane needed and sought, to make him master of his sense of immediate continuity with a world increasingly chaotic (America had lurched into the depression of the 1930s), gave Crane *The Bridge*—but in actual life did not sustain him. On his way to Mexico, he again encountered the sea; regressive symbol of the first great poems. And in Mexico, Crane was invaded subtly by a cult of death old as the Aztecs, ruthless as the sea. There was in Mexico also the will to be free of this death and of the beauty that flowers in death. Crane felt it but was only confused by this newborn groping revolutionary Mexico. The periodicity of his excesses grew swifter; the lucid intervening times when he could write were crowded out. Hart Crane fought death in Mexico. He wanted to escape. But as his boat turned toward what seemed to him the modern chaos of New York, there was the sea. And he could not resist it.

On April 27, 1932, a few moments before noon, Hart Crane walked to the stern of the *Orizaba*. The ship was about three hundred miles north of Havana, leaving the warm waters which fifteen years before he had first known and sung as a mythic haven of rest. He took off his coat quietly, and leaped.

WALDO FRANK

June 1957

NOTES

Abbreviations used in Notes:

Bridge   *The Bridge: A Poem by Hart Crane* (New York: Horace Liveright, 1930).

coll.   collected

Columbia   A collection of HC's letters, poetry, books, and memorabilia, including papers he had with him in Mexico, now in Columbia University Libraries, New York, New York.

CP   *The Collected Poems of Hart Crane*, edited with an introduction by Waldo Frank (New York: Liveright, 1933).

HC   Hart Crane

Horton   Philip Horton, *Hart Crane: The Life of an American Poet* (New York: W. W. Norton, 1937).

Key West   A collection of manuscripts and typescripts for HC's projected third volume of poetry, now in Columbia. A brief description of the *Key West* materials will be found below in the notes for "Key West: An Island Sheaf."

Letters   *The Letters of Hart Crane, 1916–1932*, edited by Brom Weber (New York: Hermitage, 1952).

Notebook   A ring-binder notebook, prepared by HC in late 1924 and early 1925, which contains versions of many poems later either included in *WB* or excluded from that volume, as well as a "commonplace-book" selection by HC of poems and poetic fragments from a number of other poets. The notebook is now in the HC collection in Columbia.

Ohio   A collection of letters and poetry sent to Gorham B. Munson by HC between August 22,

1919, and April 17, 1928, now in Ohio State
University Library, Columbus, Ohio.

pub.   published

TAY   "Hart Crane: Prose Writing," edited with an
introduction by Brom Weber (*Twice a Year*,
12–13 [Spring-Winter, 1945], pp. 424–52).

WB   *White Buildings: Poems by Hart Crane*, with
a foreword by Allen Tate (New York: Boni &
Liveright, 1926).

WB-Ms. Unpaginated, carbon-copy typescript of *White
Buildings* sent to Waldo Frank in 1926; cover
page bears a holograph note to Frank asserting
that this version is "*final*"; now in Columbia.
Page numbers in the notes below have been
assigned by the editor and enclosed in brackets.

Weber   Brom Weber, *Hart Crane: A Biographical and
Critical Study* (New York: Bodley Press,
1948).

WHITE BUILDINGS

The present text is based upon the first edition of WB; first
coll. in CP, pp. 59–110. Discrepancies between the texts of
poems in WB and CP have been collated with Notebook
and WB-Ms. Periodicals in which the affected poems appeared prior to the publication of WB have been consulted
when necessary.

SUNDAY MORNING APPLES

Stanza 4 consists of lines 15–17 (Notebook, p. 49; WB-Ms.,
p. [10]; and WB, p. 9) instead of lines 15–18 (CP, p. 67).

PRAISE FOR AN URN

Stanza 2, line 4: "of the storm." (Notebook, p. 37; WB-Ms.,
p. [11]; CP, p. 68; and the present text) corrects "of the
storm:" (WB, p. 11).

PASTORALE

Stanza 1, line 5: "her enthusiasms." (WB, p. 18) corrects
"her enthusiasms?" (CP, p. 75). The present text appears
in versions preceding CP: Notebook, p. 45; WB-Ms., p.
[15].

POSSESSIONS

Stanza 4, line 28: "the white wind rase" corrects "the white wind raze" in *CP*, p. 83. The present text occurs in versions preceding *CP*: Notebook, p. 19; *The Little Review*, 10 (Spring 1924), p. 19; WB-Ms., p. [21]; WB, p. 26.

PASSAGE

Stanza 4, line 22: "a too well-known"—in the present text and *CP* (p. 87)—is "a too well known" in WB-Ms. (p. [24]) and WB (p. 31); however, the phrase appeared as "a too well-known" in "Passage," *The Calendar*, 3 (July 1926), p. 106, so apparently the absence of a hyphen in WB-Ms. was merely a typing error carried over into WB and should not be regarded as governing.

THE WINE MENAGERIE

Stanza 5, line 19: "windowpane" corrects "window-pane" (*CP*, p. 88) and is found in versions preceding *CP*: WB-Ms., p. [25], and WB, p. 33.

Stanza 8, line 37: the present editor believes that "—Anguished the wit" (as HC had it in WB-Ms., p. [26]) is preferable to "—Anguished, the wit" (as it appears in WB, p. 33; *CP*, p. 89; and the present text), but it may be that the change from WB-Ms. to WB was not a publishing error and had been initiated by HC.

FOR THE MARRIAGE OF FAUSTUS AND HELEN I

Stanza 2, line 4: "divers dawns" (WB, p. 38; *CP*, p. 93; and the present text) is "diverse dawns" in Notebook, pp. 9, 127, and WB-Ms., p. [28].

Stanza 5, line 4: "turn dark" (Notebook, pp. 11, 129; WB-Ms., p. [29]; and WB, p. 38) corrects "turn dark," (*CP*, p. 94).

FOR THE MARRIAGE OF FAUSTUS AND HELEN II

Stanza 1, line 4: WB-Ms., p. [30], and WB, p. 40, have "opera bouffe" instead of "opéra bouffe" as in *CP*, p. 96, and the present text.

FOR THE MARRIAGE OF FAUSTUS AND HELEN III

Stanza 4 consists of lines 22–30 (WB-Ms., p. [31]; WB, p. 43; and the present text) instead of lines 31–35 (*CP*, p. 99).

Stanza 1, line 1: "—And yet" in the present text corrects "And yet" in CP, p. 102, and is derived from Notebook, p. 27; *The Little Review*, 12 (Spring-Summer 1926), p. 13; WB-Ms., p. [35]; and WB, p. 50.

Stanza 3, line 3: "poinsettia" (WB, p. 50; CP, p. 102; and the present text) was "poincetta" earlier in Notebook, p. 23; *The Little Review*, 12 (Spring-Summer 1926), p. 13; and WB-Ms., p. [35]. "Poincetta" is composed of three syllables whereas "poinsettia" may be pronounced alternately with either three or four syllables; the four-syllabic pronunciation alters the music of the line as originally written, yet the spelling correction apparently was accepted by HC when he admitted it to WB.

Stanza 2, line 9: "irrefragibly" in the present text (also in Notebook, p. 27; WB-Ms., p. [37]; WB, p. 53; CP, p. 105) is a misspelling of "irrefragably" (as it appeared correctly in *The Complete Poems of Hart Crane* [New York: Doubleday, 1958], p. 109). HC may have had the relevant adverb "irrofrangibly" in mind when he wrote "irrefragibly."

The present text also returns the poem to the five-stanza form it has in Notebook (p. 27), WB-Ms. (p. [37]), and WB (pp. 53–54), dividing the final fourth stanza in CP (pp. 105–6) between lines 16 and 17; in the present text, lines 14–16 comprise a third stanza, lines 17–23 comprise a fourth stanza, and lines 24–25 comprise a fifth stanza.

Stanza 8, line 1: "The imaged Word" in WB, p. 58; CP, p. 110; and the present text is "The imaged word" in WB-Ms., p. [39], and *The Little Review*, 12 (Spring-Summer 1926), p. 15.

THE BRIDGE

The present text is based upon the first American edition (*The Bridge: A Poem by Hart Crane* [New York: Horace Liveright, 1930]), which appeared after the first edition (Paris: Black Sun Press, 1930) and incorporates HC's revisions of that edition; first coll. in CP, pp. [1]–58.

AVE MARIA

Stanza 4, line 2: "Madre María," (*Bridge*, p. 12) corrects "Madre Maria," (*CP*, p. 6).

THE HARBOR DAWN

Stanza 4, line 6: "half-covered chair" (*Bridge*, p. 18) corrects "half-covered chair," (*CP*, p. 10).

VAN WINKLE

Stanza 2, line 1: "to school," (*Bridge*, p. 19) corrects "to school" (*CP*, p. 11); line 4: "Cortes" (*Bridge*, p. 19) corrects "Cortez" (*CP*, p. 11).

Stanza 8, line 1: "a box," (*Bridge*, p. 20) corrects "a box" (*CP*, p. 12).

THE RIVER

Stanza 2, line 9: "breathtaking" (*Bridge*, p. 22) corrects "Breathtaking" (*CP*, p. 13).

THE DANCE

Stanza 21, line 3: "thine angered" (*Bridge*, p. 31) corrects "thin angered" (*CP*, p. 22).

INDIANA

Stanza 1, line 1: "The morning glory" (*Bridge*, p. 33) corrects "The morning-glory" (*CP*, p. 24).

CUTTY SARK

Page 85: *"and turned and left us on the lee . . ."* (*Bridge*, p. 42) corrects "and turned and left us on the lee . . ." (*CP*, p. 30).

CAPE HATTERAS

Stanza 2, line 2: "Pocahontas" corrects "Pocahontus" (*Bridge*, p. 45, and *CP*, p. 31); the name was spelled "Pocahontas" in the first (Paris) edition. The spelling "Pocahontas" is used by HC in "The Dance" (stanza 4, line 2, and stanza 13, line 4) where it contrasts with the spelling "Pocahuntus" in the seventeenth-century prose epigraph to "Powhatan's Daughter," the section of *The Bridge* containing "The Dance."

Stanza 6, line 10: "new reaches" (*Bridge*, p. 48) corrects "new reaches," (*CP*, p. 34).

Stanza 10, line 19: ". . . . dispersion . . . into mashed and shapeless debris. . . ." (*Bridge*, p. 50) corrects ". . . dispersion . . . into mashed and shapeless débris. . . ." (*CP*, p. 36).

Stanza 11, line 11: "new bound" (*Bridge*, p. 51) corrects "new bound," (*CP*, p. 37).

Stanza 12, line 12: The comma in "pallid there as chalk," (*CP*, p. 37, and the present text) appeared in the first (Paris) edition but is missing in *Bridge*, p. 51; the omission appears to be a printer's error.

Stanza 17, line 7: "yes, Walt," (*Bridge*, p. 53) corrects "Yes, Walt," (*CP*, p. 39); line 9: "suddenly,–no," (*Bridge*, p. 53) corrects "suddenly,–No," (*CP*, p. 39).

THE TUNNEL
Stanza 1, line 6: "Someday" (*Bridge*, p. 71) corrects "Some day" (*CP*, p. 49).

Stanza 6, line 3: "fourth of July–" (*Bridge*, p. 72) corrects "Fourth of July–" (*CP*, p. 50).

ATLANTIS
Stanza 10, line 3: "To wrapt inception" (*Bridge*, p. 82) corrects "To rapt inception" (*CP*, p. 58); "wrapt" is a word used earlier by HC, e.g., "Voyages II" (stanza 1, line 4).

EARLY POEMS

THE MOTH THAT GOD MADE BLIND
Text from three typescript pages (Columbia) bearing holograph emendations and a concluding holograph inscription: "(Harold) Hart Crane / 25 E. 11 St. / N.Y.C. / 1915[.]" HC's slips of the pen have been corrected in stanza 3, line 12–"jewelleries" for "jeweleries"; stanza 6, line 23–"humbly" for "himbly"; stanza 10, line 38–"octopus" for "octupus." First pub., with note by Lewis Leary, in *Columbia Library Columns*, 10 (November 1960), pp. 24–26; "florescence" (stanza 7, line 26) was erroneously transcribed as "fluorescence."

C 33
First pub. in *Bruno's Weekly*, 3 (September 23, 1916), p. 1008, where the poet's name is given erroneously as "Harold H. Crone." Text from *Bruno's Weekly* with "truths" substituted for "thruths" (line 6). First coll. in

Weber, p. 381. "C 33" is apparently HC's first-known pub. poem. Gorham Munson in *Destinations* (New York: J. H. Sears, 1928, p. 163) and Waldo Frank in *CP* (p. [162]) assert that HC's first pub. poem appeared in *Bruno's Bohemia* when HC was fifteen. There is no record, however, that Guido Bruno published a *Bruno's Bohemia* before 1918, when the March issue contained HC's "Carmen de Boheme."

OCTOBER-NOVEMBER
First pub. as by "Harold H. Crane" in *The Pagan*, 1 (November-December 1916), p. 33, from which text has been taken. First coll. in *CP*, p. 168, where year of publication is given erroneously as 1918 and line 2 is partially erroneous ("mists,—" instead of "mists;").

THE HIVE
First pub. as by "Harold Crane" in *The Pagan*, 1 (March 1917), p. 36, from which text has been taken. First coll. in *CP*, p. 163, where line 6 is partially erroneous ("forth;" instead of "forth.").

FEAR
First pub. as by "Harold H. Crane" in *The Pagan*, 1-2 (April-May 1917), p. 11, from which text has been taken. First coll. in *CP*, p. 169, where year of publication is given erroneously as 1918 and line 1 is partially erroneous ("well" instead of "well,").

ANNUNCIATIONS
First pub. as by "Harold H. Crane" in *The Pagan*, 1-2 (April-May 1917), p. 11, from which text has been taken. First coll. in *CP*, p. 164, with alterations in lines 6 ("sand" instead of "sound"), 7 ("moan" instead of "moans"—"in" instead of "of"), and 8 ("withdrawn" instead of "outdrawn").

ECHOES
First pub. in *The Pagan*, 2 (October-November 1917), p. 39, from which text has been taken. First coll. in Weber, pp. 381–82. "Slivers" (line 1) was misspelled "slivvers" in *The Pagan*.

THE BATHERS
First pub. in *The Pagan*, 2 (December 1917), p. 19, from

which text has been taken. First coll. in *CP*, p. 165, with alterations in lines 4 ("hear" instead of "hear,"), 5 ("sound—" instead of "sound,—"), and 11 ("Silence" instead of "silence").

MODERN CRAFT

First pub. in *The Pagan*, 2 (January 1918), p. 37; first coll. in *CP*, p. 166. A spelling correction in *CP* ("lilies" for "lillies" [line 5]) has been followed in the present text.

CARMEN DE BOHEME

First pub. as by "Harold H. Crane" in *Bruno's Bohemia*, 1 (March 1918), p. 2, from which text has been taken. First coll. in Weber, pp. 382–83, with line 12 partially erroneous ("soft-pulling:—and" instead of "soft-pulling:———and").

CARRIER LETTER

First pub. in *The Pagan*, 2-3 (April-May 1918), p. 20; first coll. in *CP*, p. 167, with line 8 partially erroneous ("your tryst-ring" instead of "the tryst-ring").

POSTSCRIPT

First pub. in *The Pagan*, 2-3 (April-May 1918), p. 20; first coll. in *CP*, p. 170. The present text, derived from Notebook, p. 89, differs from preceding versions by revising line 2 ("light and pain" instead of "light, and pain").

FORGETFULNESS

First pub. in *The Pagan*, 3 (August-September 1918), p. 15, from which text has been taken. First coll. in *CP*, p. 172, where a comma was omitted in line 4 ("motionless—" instead of "motionless,—") and line 8 was broken erroneously into two lines ("Forgetfulness is white,— / White as a blasted tree,").

TO PORTAPOVITCH

First pub. as "To Potapovitch" in *The Modern School*, 6 (March 1919), p. 80. First coll. under same title in *CP*, p. 171 (subtitle gives "of the Ballet Russe" instead of "de la Ballet Russe" as in first publication and line 4 also erroneously gives "won;—" instead of "won:—"). Text and title from HC's final draft in Notebook, p. 63, which duplicates lines of first publication but corrects spelling of title and replaces "de la" in the subtitle with "du." HC's table of contents in Notebook, p. 93, also cites the poem as "To Portapovitch." Stanislaw Portapovitch was a dancer; an advertisement for his school of dance appeared in *The Little Review*, 6 (June 1919).

LEGENDE

First pub. in *The Modernist*, 3 (November 1919), p. 28; first coll. in Weber, pp. 383–84, with errors in lines 2 ("her" instead of "her."), 7 ("sands" instead of "sand"), and 8 ("Spring" instead of "spring"). Present text taken from Notebook, p. 59, which revises the *Modernist* text in line 7 ("sand and sea" instead of "sand and the sea").

INTERIOR

First pub. in *The Modernist*, 3 (November 1919), p. 28; first coll. in Weber, p. 383. Text from Notebook, p. 57; this contains HC's final draft and it revises earlier drafts of lines appearing in the two previously published versions: lines 1 ("It is a shy solemnity,"), 2 ("This lamp in our small room."), and 8 ("Here in the curtained glow").

EPISODE OF HANDS

First pub. in Weber, p. 384. Text, which agrees with that in Weber, has been taken from a microfilm copy of a typescript page (Ohio) sent to Gorham Munson, April 26, 1920.

THE BRIDGE OF ESTADOR

First pub. in Weber, p. 385. Text from microfilm copies of two typescript pages (Ohio) sent to Gorham Munson, April 10, 1921; it conforms to Weber text with several exceptions ("perhaps," replaces "perhaps" [line 3]; "before." replaces "before," [line 14]; "awaiting" replaces "Awaiting" [line 19]; "dreams. . . ." replaces "dreams . . ." [line 21]; "Of things" replaces "of things" [line 23]; "among stars." replaces "among the stars." [line 28]).

PORPHYRO IN AKRON

First pub. in *The Double Dealer*, 2 (August-September 1921), p. 53; first coll. in Weber, pp. 386–87, with several errors. Present text taken from Notebook, pp. 71, 73, and 75, which revises the *Double Dealer* text in section I (line 1: "dawn," instead of "dawn"; line 4: "stubborness"—a spelling error corrected in present text—instead of "stubbornness"; line 6: "cars" instead of "cars,"; line 10: "place',—" instead of "place,'—"; line 11: "smoke-ridden hills" instead of "smoking hills"); in section II (line 5: "gentlemen',—" instead of "gentlemen,'—"; creates a new, third stanza consisting of lines 8–12; line 9: "horse. . . . Have" instead of "horse . . . Have"); and in section III (lines 12–13 in present text created from line 12: "To find the only rose on the bush in the front yard."; line 14: "Porphyro,—your" instead of "Porphyro—your").

Section III, line 4: "Madeline's" (Weber, p. 386, and present text) corrects "Madeleine's" (*The Double Dealer*, p. 53, and Notebook, p. 75), thus bringing lines 3–5 of this section into conformity with their source (John Keats, "The Eve of St. Agnes," stanza xxv, lines 1–3).

A PERSUASION

First pub. in *The Measure*, no. 8 (October 1921), p. 14, from which text has been taken. First coll. in Weber, pp. 387–88 (line 10 erroneously gives "morning," instead of "morning").

LOCUTIONS DES PIERROTS

First pub. in *The Double Dealer*, 3 (May 1922), pp. 261–62, from which text has been taken. First coll. in Weber, pp. 388–89, with three errors (I, stanza 1, line 4: "affections." instead of "affections?"; I, stanza 3, line 4: "sharing" instead of "snaring"; III, stanza 3, line 4: "Your sex!" instead of "Your Sex!").

THE GREAT WESTERN PLAINS

First pub. in *Gargoyle*, 3 (August 1922), unpaged, from which text has been taken. First coll. in Weber, pp. 389–90.

AMERICA'S PLUTONIC ECSTASIES

First pub. in *S4N*, 4 (May-August 1923), unpaged, from which the text has been taken ("prefering" in line 1 has been corrected to "preferring"). First coll. in Weber, pp. 390–91.

INTERLUDIUM

First pub. in 1924, 1 (July 1924), p. 2; first coll. in Weber, pp. 393–94. The present text has been taken from Notebook, p. 79.

KEY WEST: AN ISLAND SHEAF

HC contemplated a collection of his poems to be entitled "Key West: An Island Sheaf" and had progressed so far as to prepare a title page that included the three-line epigraph from William Blake. He had also prepared a table of contents which, together with the manuscripts of several poems, he kept in a file folder that was with him in Mexico in 1932. The folder, labeled "KEY WEST" by HC, is now in Columbia. The folder's contents are not in the final typed form customarily prepared for a publisher, thus making it clear that the projected book had not been made ready for publication at the time of HC's death in April 1932. Consequently, there can be no certainty that the poems contained in the folder would have been included in the completed book nor indeed that other poems would not have found their way into it. The *Key West* poems have been presented here as uncollected material rather than as the completed works they were purported to be in CP. Such a procedure does justice to HC's meticulous sense of self-criticism and to his habit of frequent revision; it clearly indicates the tentative state of the collection when considered as a book ready for publication.

HC's table of contents lists thirteen poems in the following order: "O Carib Isle!," "The Mermen," "To the Cloud Juggler," "The Mango Tree," "Island Quarry," "Old Song," "The Idiot," "A Name for All," "Connecticut-Cubano Overheard" ["Bacardi Spreads the Eagle's Wings"], "Imperator Victus," "Royal Palm," "The Air Plant," and "The Hour!" ["The Hurricane"]. The poems appear in this edition in the same order, though "The Hurricane"—a revision of "The Hour!"—replaces it.

The *Key West* folder also contains drafts of eight other poems: "The Tree: Great William," "To Shakespeare," "Key West," "The Hurricane," "By Nilus Once I Knew . . . ," "Moment Fugue," and "To Emily Dickinson." Whether or not HC placed these in the folder, or whether they were placed there later by other hands, is a matter for conjecture. Since "To Shakespeare" is a revision of "The Tree: Great William," the latter has been excluded from this edition.

The remaining poems have been grouped in approximate chronological order and follow the poems HC listed on his contents page.

O CARIB ISLE!

First pub. in *transition*, no. 1 (April 1927), pp. 101–2; first coll. in *CP*, pp. 114–15. Several variant versions of this poem exist. Text has been taken from HC's last draft, a typescript page with holograph emendation in *Key West*, which also provided the text in *CP* (except that "fiddler" was substituted in *CP* for "fiddle" [line 3]; "the" substituted for "this" [line 17]; "of the mildew" substituted for "of mildew" [line 21]; one whole line, "And clenched beaks coughing for the surge again!" omitted [line 31]; and "on" substituted for "of" [line 32]).

THE MERMEN

First pub. in *The Dial*, 85 (July 1928), p. 230; first coll. in *CP*, p. 118. Text has been taken from HC's last draft (typescript page in *Key West*), which also furnished the text in *CP* (except that "His" was substituted erroneously for "this" [line 14], "face" substituted for "Face" [line 15], and the typographical arrangement of the poem not followed in two details).

TO THE CLOUD JUGGLER

First pub. in *transition*, nos. 19–20 (June 1930), p. 223; first coll. in *CP*, pp. 130–31. Text from a carbon-copy typescript page (bearing holograph note: "Sent to Caresse [Crosby] / January 23rd [1930]") in *Key West*, which also provided the text in *CP* (except that "sealight" was substituted erroneously for "sleight" in line 10).

THE MANGO TREE

First pub. in *transition*, no. 18 (November 1929), p. 95; first coll. in *CP*, p. 116. Text from a typescript page in *Key West*, which also furnished the text in *CP* (except that "musical hanging jug" was substituted for "musical, hanging jug" [line 4] and "you sun-heap" substituted for "you Sun-heap" [line 12]).

ISLAND QUARRY

First pub. in *transition*, no. 9 (December 1927), p. 132;

first coll. in *CP*, p. 117 (where "marble into" was substituted for "marble only into" [line 1] and "In dusk it" substituted for "In dusk, it" [line 8]). The poem is the first of a group of five appearing together in *transition*, no. 9, pp. 132–36, under the collective title of "East of Yucatan": "Island Quarry," "Royal Palm," "Overheard" ["Bacardi Spreads the Eagle's Wings"], "El Idiota" ["The Idiot"], and "The Hour" ["The Hurricane"]. Present text taken from a typescript page (*Key West*) which revises the *transition* version in line 2 ("Flat prison slabs" instead of "Flat slabs") and line 8 ("In dusk, as though" instead of "In dusk, it is at times as though").

OLD SONG

First pub. in *The New Republic*, 51 (August 10, 1927), p. 309; first coll. in *CP*, p. 139. Text from a typescript page (*Key West*), which conforms in all details but one minor punctuation variant ("rose,–" instead of "rose–" [line 1]) with the first published version; bears the typed notation of "New Republic / Aug. '27"; and corrects the version in *CP* by giving "Thy absence" instead of "Thine absence" (line 1), "the dream." instead of "the dream" (line 4), and "burden of the" instead of "burden on the" (line 9).

THE IDIOT

First pub. in *transition*, no. 9 (December 1927), p. 135 (see note for "Island Quarry"); first coll. in *CP*, p. 119. Text from a typescript page (*Key West*) with holograph emendations entitled "The Idiot," which also furnished text in *CP* (except that "see" was substituted in *CP* for "see–" [line 1], "That boy" substituted for "The boy" [line 2], and "kite string;" substituted for "kite string," [line 9]).

A NAME FOR ALL

First pub. in *The Dial*, 86 (April 1929), p. 297; first coll. in *CP*, p. 120.

BACARDI SPREADS THE EAGLE'S WINGS

First pub. as "Overheard" in *transition*, no. 9 (December 1927), p. 134 (see note for "Island Quarry"); first pub. as "Bacardi Spreads the Eagle's Wings" in *Contempo*, 2 (July 5, 1932), p. 1; first coll. in *CP*, p. 126. Text from *Con-*

tempo, to which HC sent the poem on March 11, 1932; it differs from text in *CP* (apparently an erroneous transcription of the *Contempo* version combined with some of the punctuation in the earlier *transition* version).

IMPERATOR VICTUS

First pub. in *Poetry,* 41 (January 1933), p. 180; first coll. in *CP,* p. 123. Text from a typescript page (*Key West*) with holograph emendations, which also provided text for *CP* (where lines 11, 12, and 13 were omitted).

ROYAL PALM

First pub. in *transition,* no. 9 (December 1927), p. 133 (see note for "Island Quarry"); first coll. in *CP,* p. 121. The text has been taken from *transition,* which apparently also furnished text in *CP* (except that "more than regal" was substituted for "more-than-regal" [line 1] and "aethereal" for "aetherial" [line 8]).

THE AIR PLANT

First pub. in *The Dial,* 84 (January 1928), p. 140. First coll. in *CP,* p. 122, whose text is taken from a typescript page (*Key West*) bearing notation "Hart Crane, / RFD-Patterson, N.Y. / no cent to Criterion / July 16th." The present text conforms to that in *CP.*

THE HURRICANE

First pub. as "The Hour" in *transition,* no. 9 (December 1927), p. 136 (see note for "Island Quarry"); first pub. as "The Hurricane" in *The New Republic,* 67 (July 29, 1931), p. 277. First coll. in *CP,* pp. 124–25, where the text is based on a typescript page (*Key West*) with holograph emendations that precedes the *New Republic* version, from which the present text has been taken.

TO EMILY DICKINSON

First pub. in *The Nation,* 124 (June 29, 1927), p. 718. First coll. in *CP,* p. 128, whose text is based on a typescript page (*Key West*) with a holograph emendation ("Needs" instead of "Takes" in line 11) that provides the only variation from the *Nation* text. The present text conforms to that in *CP.*

KEY WEST

First pub. in *CP*, p. 113, whose text was derived from a typescript page with holograph emendations (*Key West*) embodying the latest known version of the poem. There are two other versions of the poem in *Key West*: (1) the earliest draft is on a holograph page; (2) an intermediate draft is on a typescript page with holograph emendations. The present text follows that in *CP*. It should be noted that line 13 in the manuscript appears to the present editor to have been left in an unfinished state by HC; other readers may disagree.

—AND BEES OF PARADISE

First pub. as "And Bees of Paradise" in *The New Republic*, 74 (February 15, 1933), p. 16. First coll. in *CP*, p. 127, whose text is derived from a typescript page (*Key West*) with holograph emendations dated "7/28/27." The present text conforms to that in *CP*, but the title has been revised to accord with the typescript.

MOMENT FUGUE

First pub. in *transition*, no. 15 (February 1929), p. 102; first coll. in *CP*, p. 129. The present text has been taken from a typescript page (*Key West*) which apparently provided the text in *CP* (except that "the flesh" was substituted for "no flesh" in line 15).

BY NILUS ONCE I KNEW . . .

First pub. in *Poetry*, 41 (January 1933), p. 184; first coll. in *CP*, p. 132. The text has been taken from a typescript page (*Key West*) with holograph emendations and differs from the *CP* text (derived from the same typescript) in several lines ("the air," instead of "the air" [line 1]; "lowly shed." instead of "lonely shed." [line 4]; "plight:" instead of "plight" [line 7]).

MORE LATE POEMS

Poems written after 1925 which were not published either in *WB* or *Bridge* and were not included by HC in his projected "Key West: An Island Sheaf."

THE VISIBLE THE UNTRUE

First pub. in *Poetry*, 41 (January 1933), pp. 182–83. First coll. in *CP*, pp. 148–49. The present text, derived from a typescript page (Columbia) bearing holograph emendations and apparently also the basis of the *CP* text, replaces "in two" with "in two[,]" (line 4); "your sanctions?" with "what sanctions—?" (line 14); and "the day of unkind farewell." with "the farewell day unkind." (line 23). Several of HC's typing errors, such as "terribel" and "Zepplin," have been silently corrected.

REPLY

First pub. in *Poetry*, 41 (January 1933), pp. 183–84; first coll. in *CP*, p. 154, whose text was derived from an untitled typescript page (Columbia). The page bears a holograph note by Samuel Loveman, who assisted Waldo Frank in preparing *CP*, indicating that Loveman gave the poem its title. Present text has been taken from the typescript and replaces "appetite," with "appetite" (line 1).

THE PHANTOM BARK

First pub. in *Poetry*, 41 (January 1933), p. 185. First coll. in *CP*, p. 137, with a text apparently derived from a typescript page (Columbia) entitled "fragment note" and bearing holograph emendations in the last line. The *CP* text properly corrected HC's slip of the pen (line 2) in writing "men" instead of "man" but, inexplicably, replaced "adream" with "a-dream" (line 4) and "steam" with "rain" (line 12). The last line of the manuscript is unfinished; *CP* gave it the following reading: "Imprisoned never, no not soot or rain."

LENSES

First pub. in Weber, p. 396. Text from a typescript page (Columbia) and is identical with Weber text. The typescript bears a heading indicating that the poem was intended for *The Bridge*: "(directly preceding Tunnel) / VII or VIII / LENSES." A large transparent "X" drawn over the typescript suggests that HC rejected the poem as a part of *The Bridge*, in which it does not appear.

TO LIBERTY

First pub. in Weber, pp. 396–97. Text has been taken from a typescript page (Columbia) with seven fragmentary holograph lines below two typed stanzas and differs from Weber text in excluding the holograph lines.

ETERNITY

First pub. in *The New Republic*, 74 (February 15, 1933), pp. 15–16; first coll. in *CP*, pp. 156–58. Text, from two typescript pages (Columbia) with holograph emendations, differs only slightly from that in *CP* ("Negroes" was substituted erroneously for "negroes" [line 12]).

TO THE EMPRESS JOSEPHINE'S STATUE

First pub. in Weber, p. 398, from a faulty transcription. The present text is derived from two holograph pages (Columbia) on which "Caribbean" was misspelled.

A POSTSCRIPT

First pub. in *Poetry*, 41 (January 1933), pp. 185–86; first coll. in *CP*, p. 155. The present text is based on a typescript page (Columbia) with numerous holograph emendations, apparently the source of the *CP* text, but differs from the *CP* text by replacing "towards" with "toward" (line 6); "lavender of that dawn, lilies" with "lavender lilies of that dawn," (line 7); "desert, and" with "desert and" (line 10); and "porters, jokes" with "porters[,] jokes" (line 11). The content suggests that the poem was written after HC's return from Cuba in 1926.

TO SHAKESPEARE

First pub. in *The New Republic*, 74 (April 5, 1933), p. 212; first coll. in *CP*, p. 133. The present text is based on a typescript page (Columbia) with holograph emendations, apparently also the source of the *CP* text, but differs from the *CP* text by replacing "fate," with "fate[,]" (line 8) and "And fall," with "—And fail," (line 12). An earlier draft, entitled "The Tree: Great William," appeared in *CP*, pp. 133–34; it belongs in a complete variorum edition of HC's poems.

MARCH

First pub. in *larus: The Celestial Visitor*, 1 (March 1927), p. 14; first coll. in *CP*, p. 138.

HAVANA ROSE

First pub. in *Poetry*, 41 (January 1933), pp. 180–82; first coll. in *CP*, pp. 152–53. The present text is taken from two holograph pages (Columbia) apparently the source of the *CP* text, but differs from that text in several lines (numbered as they appear on pp. 188–89 of present edition) by replacing "house" with "horse" (1); "wind, that" with "wind that" (5); "doors, and the watchman" with "trundle doors, and the cherub watchman—" (6–7); "balconies trundling with" with "balconies with" (7–8); "to cure" with "*to cure*" (15); "supposedly" with "*supposedly*" (16–17); "again,—" with "again—" (23); "courage," with "courage" (25); "American" with "American," (30); "negative," with "negative—" (31); and "birth." with "birth.["]" (35). The four paragraphs of the *CP* text have been combined into two to conform with the manuscripts.

RELIQUARY
First pub. in *Poetry*, 41 (January 1933), pp. 177–78; first coll. in *CP*, p. 150. The present text has been taken from an untitled holograph page (Columbia), apparently the source of the *CP* text, but differs from that text in several lines by replacing "resolution!" with "resolution[!]" (1); "pillow," with "pillow—" (2); "Sagittarius," with "Sagittarius" (5); "those who are variants," with "(those who are variants[)]" (8); "Time?—Who" with "time—who" (14); and "defends?" with "defends . . . [?]" (17). A new stanza begins at line 9 to conform with the manuscript.

PURGATORIO
First pub. in *Poetry*, 41 (January 1933), p. 178; first coll. in *CP*, p. 151. The present text has been taken from two holograph pages (Columbia) apparently the source of the *CP* text, but differs from that text in several lines by replacing "grow?" with "grow[?]" (10); "stall;" with "stall[.]" (12); "thus purgatory—not such as Dante built," with "thus a purgatory—not such as Dante built" (13); "quilt," with "quilt—" (14); "town?" with "town[?]" (16); "anew," with "anew[,]" (17); "As ring" with "So ring" (18); "heed" with "need" (19); "time, was not so." with "time was not [. . .]" (21).

THE SAD INDIAN
First pub. in *Poetry*, 41 (January 1933), p. 182; first coll.

291

in CP, p. 145. The present text has been taken from a holograph page (Columbia) apparently the source of the CP text, but varies from that text in several lines by replacing "his woof" with "the woof" (3); "vantage and" with "vantage—and" (5); and "Their shadows" with "—Their shadows" (8).

THE BROKEN TOWER
First pub. in *The New Republic*, 71 (June 8, 1932), p. 91; first coll. in CP, pp. 135–36, whose text corrects the *New Republic* version by replacing "town" with "tower" (stanza 2, line 2). The CP text conforms to typescripts of the poem sent at Easter 1932 to Samuel Loveman (Columbia) and Malcolm Cowley (Yale University Library) with two exceptions: "intervals. . . ." instead of "intervals . . ." (stanza 3, line 4) and "pebbles—visible" instead of "pebbles,—visible" (stanza 9, line 3).

SELECTED PROSE

THE CASE AGAINST NIETZSCHE
First pub. in *The Pagan*, 2-3 (April-May 1918), pp. 34–35; first coll. in TAY, pp. 426–27.

JOYCE AND ETHICS
Letter first pub. in *The Little Review*, 5 (July 1918), p. 65; first coll. in TAY, pp. 427–28.

REVIEW OF *The Ghetto and Other Poems*
Review of Lola Ridge's *The Ghetto and Other Poems* (New York: Huebsch, 1918); first pub. as "The Ghetto and Other Poems / By Lola Ridge," *The Pagan*, 3 (January 1919), pp. 55–56; first coll. in TAY, pp. 428–30.

REVIEW OF *Minna and Myself*
Review of Maxwell Bodenheim's *Minna and Myself* (New York: Pagan, 1918); first pub. as "Minna and Myself," *The Pagan*, 3 (February 1919), pp. 59–60; first coll. in TAY, pp. 430–31.

REVIEW OF *Winesburg, Ohio*
Review of Sherwood Anderson's *Winesburg, Ohio* (New York: Huebsch, 1919); first pub. as "Sherwood Anderson,"

The Pagan, 4 (September 1919), pp. 60–61; first coll. in *TAY*, pp. 431–33.

A NOTE ON MINNS

First pub. in *The Little Review*, 7 (September-December 1920), p. 60, as an introduction to three photographs by H. W. Minns; first coll. in *TAY*, p. 433.

SHERWOOD ANDERSON

First pub. in *The Double Dealer*, 2 (July 1921), pp. 42–45; first coll. in *TAY*, pp. 433–38.

REVIEW OF *Eight More Harvard Poets*

Review of *Eight More Harvard Poets*, eds., S. Foster Damon and Robert Hillyer (New York: Brentano's, 1923); first pub. as "Eight More Harvard Poets," *S4N*, 4 (March-April 1923), unpaged; first coll. in *TAY*, pp. 438–39.

GENERAL AIMS AND THEORIES

First pub. in Horton, pp. 323–28. The essay is apparently the set of "notes" prepared by HC in 1925 for Eugene O'Neill to aid O'Neill in writing a foreword for the projected *White Buildings*; see letter 234 to Gorham Munson, March 17, 1926, in *Letters*, p. 240 (reprinted in the present edition).

A LETTER TO GORHAM MUNSON

First pub. in Horton, pp. 341–45. The present text differs from that in Horton and has been taken from the version in *Letters*, pp. 237–40, derived from the original typescript (Ohio). The letter is a response to Munson's essay on HC in *Destinations: A Canvass of American Literature since 1900* (New York: J. H. Sears, 1928, pp. 160–73); HC's other, later comments upon the essay will be found in *Letters*, pp. 323–24. "Allen" is Allen Tate.

A LETTER TO WALDO FRANK

First pub. in *Letters*, pp. 260–62: the last two paragraphs (p. 262) have not been reprinted. For a more complete view of HC's response to Spengler's *The Decline of the West*, and of the relatively brief period during which HC remained depressed by that work and by unrelated but equally disturbing personal circumstances, see his letters from May 22, 1926, to August 19, 1926, in *Letters*, pp. 254–74.

A LETTER TO HARRIET MONROE

First pub. in *Poetry*, 29 (October 1926), pp. 35–39, as part of an interchange of correspondence (pp. 35–41) with Harriet Monroe, the editor, regarding "At Melville's Tomb," which appeared in the same issue (p. 25). First coll. in Horton, pp. 329–34.

A LETTER TO YVOR WINTERS

First pub. partially in Horton, pp. 224–26; first pub. fully in *Letters*, pp. 298–302, from which present text has been taken. The article by Edmund Wilson referred to by HC is "The Muses Out of Work," *The New Republic*, 50 (May 11, 1927), pp. 319–21.

A LETTER TO OTTO H. KAHN

First pub. with deletions in *The Hound & Horn*, 7 (July-September 1934), pp. 679–82. First coll. in Horton, pp. 335–40. The present text differs from the two earlier publications and is taken from the version in *Letters*, pp. 304–9, derived from the carbon-copy typescript of HC's original typewritten letter (Columbia). A shortened and somewhat revised version of this letter (Columbia) was prepared by HC after 1927 (see HC to Paul Rosenfeld and Eda Lou Walton, *Letters*, pp. 350–51).

A LETTER TO HERBERT WEINSTOCK

First pub. in *Letters*, pp. 350–51; the final paragraph (p. 351) has not been reprinted. Weinstock's review of *The Bridge* appeared in the Milwaukee *Journal*, April 12, 1930.

A LETTER TO ALLEN TATE

First pub. partially in Horton, pp. 267–69. The present fuller text comes from *Letters*, pp. 352–54; the last paragraph (p. 354) has not been reprinted. The publications to which HC refers include: Genevieve Taggard, "The Process behind Poetry," New York *Herald-Tribune* "Books," July 13, 1930, p. 2; Allen Tate, "A Distinguished Poet," *The Hound & Horn*, 3 (July-September 1930), pp. 580–85; Yvor Winters, "Poetry, Morality, and Criticism," in *The Critique of Humanism: A Symposium*, ed., C. Hartley Grattan (New York: Brewer and Warren, 1930), pp. 301–33; Yvor Winters, "The Progress of Hart Crane," *Poetry*, 36 (June 1930), pp. 153–63.

MODERN POETRY

First pub. in Oliver M. Sayler, *Revolt in the Arts: A Survey of the Creation, Distribution and Appreciation of Art in America* (New York: Brentano's, 1930), pp. 294–98, from which the present text has been taken. First coll. in *CP*, pp. 175–79, with some alterations, the only significant one being the substitution of "liberation" for "liberating" in the second paragraph (last sentence) of the essay.

FROM HAUNTS OF PROSERPINE

Review of James Whaler's *Green River: A Poem for Rafinesque* (New York: Harcourt, Brace & Co., 1931); first pub. in *Poetry*, 40 (April 1932), pp. 44–47; first coll. in *TAY*, pp. 446–49.

APPENDIX

HART CRANE, BY WALDO FRANK

First pub. as "Foreword," *The Complete Poems of Hart Crane*, ed., Waldo Frank (Garden City, N.Y.: Doubleday Anchor, 1958), pp. xi–xvi. The essay is an abridged version of the Introduction to *CP*, pp. vii–xxix.

INDEX OF FIRST LINES

297

INDEX OF TITLES
(Asterisks denote prose works)

299